WORLD RELIGIONS
IN SEVEN SENTENCES

A SMALL INTRODUCTION TO A VAST TOPIC

DOUGLAS GROOTHUIS

Academic
An imprint of InterVarsity Press
Downers Grove, Illinois

InterVarsity Press
P.O. Box 1400 | Downers Grove, IL 60515-1426
ivpress.com | email@ivpress.com

Cover design: David Fassett
Interior design: Daniel van Loon

ISBN 978-1-5140-0582-8 (print) | ISBN 978-1-5140-0583-5 (digital)

Printed in the United States of America ∞

Library of Congress Cataloging-in-Publication Data
A catalog record for this book is available from the Library of Congress.

29   28   27   26   25   24   23 | 13   12   11   10   9   8   7   6   5   4   3   2   1

To James W. Sire,

who taught me to think in terms of worldviews.

CONTENTS

ACKNOWLEDGMENTS

My thanks to my editor at IVP Academic, David McNutt, for his patience and insights on this manuscript and to my wife, Kathleen, for her support and encouragement in my ministry. Although he did not write primarily on comparative religion, the late James Sire has helped me greatly in approaching religions in terms of their worldview.

INTRODUCTION

JUST SEVEN SENTENCES?

Although I have written a small book on a vast topic using the trope of "seven sentences" called *Philosophy in Seven Sentences*, I think it is still fitting to defend and explain this idiosyncratic method.[1] One defense is that my publisher has released a few other titles using the same sevenfold strategy for other disciplines and—I hope in good judgment—gave me a contract for this book. But there is more.

First, we need to know something—beyond clichés—about religion and the major world religions to be good neighbors. Steve Prothero underscored this a few years ago in *Religious Literacy*, which—in a more curmudgeonly fashion—could have been called *Religious Illiteracy*.[2] He rightly claimed that Americans are more religious than Europeans but know less about religion than their generally irreligious counterparts across the pond. His book admirably addressed and endeavored to correct this unfortunate American ignorance. I hope this book will do so as well.

Second, while one can find vast tomes on particular religions and on how religions differ and relate to each other, not all of us

---

[1]Douglas Groothuis, *Philosophy in Seven Sentences: A Short Introduction to a Vast Topic* (Downers Grove, IL: IVP Academic, 2016).
[2]Stephen Prothero, *Religious Literacy: What Every American Needs to Know—And Doesn't* (New York: HarperOne, 2008).

have the wherewithal to read such lengthy volumes. Thus, we find a need for a responsible and concise introduction to the major world religions. While the "for dummies" approach will be resisted, this book does not assume much previous knowledge of world religions, nor will it be encumbered by weighty academic prose or scholarly apparatus. However, the footnotes will document key claims and can be used to lead readers into deeper waters without fear of drowning.

The seven sentences idea uses particular and paradigmatic statements from the world religions—and one from the irreligious Nietzsche, representing atheism—as windows into their worldviews and ways of life. My angle is more from the philosophy of religion than from the psychology or history of religion, but these elements—and others—will come into view. The sentence approach is meant not as a reduction of any religion to a mere statement but rather as an entry point of intellectual exploration. Nor would adherents of the religions I address necessarily choose my statements as the best representations of their religions. Part of the challenge—and fun—of these volumes is selecting just one sentence to represent a broad religious or philosophical tradition. I'm sure that some would chose other sentences, but I hope that my selections will be helpful.

Third, since I have taught a course called Religious Pluralism at Denver Seminary since the early 1990s, as well as taught about religions in other settings for even longer, I hope my background and interests are adequate to the task. Moreover, my approach to apologetics—whether in writing or in teaching—has always involved the relationship of Christianity to other religions.[3]

---

[3]See Douglas Groothuis, *Christian Apologetics: A Comprehensive Case for Biblical Faith*, 2nd ed. (Downers Grove, IL: IVP Academic, 2022).

Contrast is the mother of clarity. Notwithstanding, my interest is more than academic since I have had conversations and dialogues with many adherents of religions outside my own. While knowing about religions is necessary for engaging religious people rightly, and especially "religious others," it is not sufficient for a kind interaction. A "religious other" is a rather impersonal and sociological-sounding phrase for a person—who is made in the image of God—who does not share your religious commitments. However, the religious other is anything but impersonal or abstract.

Play Fair

We ought to adhere to the golden rule taught by Jesus to treat others the way we would want them to treat us (Mt 7:12). Just as a Christian would not want one of another religion, or no religion, to misrepresent Christianity, so too Christians should strive to properly represent other religions and open a listening ear to their adherents. All humility aside, years ago I was delighted when, after a lecture on Buddhism and Christianity, a young man told me that I had given the clearest and fairest description of Buddhism that he had heard. He had been raised a Buddhist. I had gone on to challenge Buddhism in light of Christ's identity and teaching, but he was still appreciative. That is my aim.

While Christians are justifiably concerned that those in other religions or no religion discover the truth of the gospel and experience the severe goodness of life in Christ, their interactions will include much more than bearing Christian witness, doing apologetics, and evangelism (although those should not be minimized). We should be civil in a religiously pluralistic society. *Pluralism*, in this sense, does not mean claiming that all religions are equally good or true or that religions can somehow be fit into a larger viewpoint in which they are all deemed equally legitimate as roads to salvation.[4] That is an unsupportable philosophical claim, which I will briefly address in another chapter. Here, *pluralism* is taken in a sociological and political sense, with descriptive and normative elements. First to the descriptive element.

Pluralism and Religious Liberty

The roots and general character of America and Western civilization in general have been Judeo-Christian, with the majority of Americans being or at least identifying as Christian. However, Judaism has contributed not only religious adherents but also contributed much to the political philosophy of the American founding.[5] However, given the First Amendment's brilliant balance of neither establishing any national religion nor prohibiting the free exercise of religion, American commitment to religious liberty—however imperfectly discharged—has created a country in which no religion is prescribed and no religion is proscribed. This, along with liberal legal immigration policies, has led to a nation that is legally friendly to diverse religions.

In many American cities, we find numerous churches across many denominations, as well as religious worship places for Jews, Hindus, Buddhists, Muslims, and others. As sociologists Roger Finke and Rodney Stark have noted, the American political arrangement for religion has led to the flourishing of various religions, all of which must compete with one another

---

[4]See Douglas Groothuis, "Religious Pluralism: Many Religions, One Truth," in *Christian Apologetics*; and Harold A. Netland, *Christianity and Religious Diversity* (Grand Rapids, MI: Baker Academic, 2015).

[5]See Os Guinness, *The Magna Carta of Humanity* (Downers Grove, IL: InterVarsity Press, 2021).

for adherents.[6] There is no established church. Nor is there the official enforcement of secularism, as was true in the former Union of Soviet Socialist Republics (USSR) and in China today. Religions in America, therefore, must be entrepreneurial to gain followers. Consequently, we face the *fact* of religious pluralism in America.

Given what I've said about the First Amendment, we should likewise value religious pluralism on the political level. This is the normative dimension of pluralism. Although Christians cannot endorse other religions as conduits of salvation, they can affirm the right of all Americans to practice any religion or no religion. That is how the United States as a republic ought to be ordered. Just as we desire religious liberty, so too we should desire it for others. Christianity, properly understood, should be propagated by persuasion, not by coercion or by legal or political pressure of any kind. Jesus bid his followers to disciple the nations by teaching them what Jesus had taught them (Mt 28:18-20). Paul should be the Christian's example.

> Rather, we have renounced secret and shameful ways; we do not use deception, nor do we distort the word of God. On the contrary, by setting forth the truth plainly we commend ourselves to everyone's conscience in the sight of God. (2 Cor 4:2)

We should wince, pray, and act when we hear of the suppression of any religion in any country, not because we equally value all religion but because we endorse freedom of conscience and the freedom of religion. The very notion of freedom of conscience and religion is traced to Christian roots, which in turn

---

[6]Roger Finke and Rodney Stark, *The Churching of America, 1776–2005: Winners and Losers in Our Religious Economy*, rev. ed. (New Brunswick, NJ: Rutgers University Press, 2005).

have borne fruit in Western history, and especially in America, as Robert Wilken has persuasively argued in *Liberty in the Things of God*.[7]

Not only should we support religious liberty for all as well as aiming for an accurate understanding of other religions, but we should also seek to be civil and even compassionate with religious others. If our fellow students, coworkers, and neighbors are adherents of a religion other than our own, it behooves us to know something about their beliefs and to treat them with civility. You don't offer a Muslim a glass of wine, for example. Since most Hindus do not eat meat, it is best not to invite them to a barbeque (unless there is a meat substitute available). Love of neighbor demands that we be polite and respectful of anyone's religion, including how we act at a Jewish funeral, a Hindu wedding, or any number of other events to which we may be welcomed.[8]

TRUTH IS ONE, RELIGIONS ARE MANY

Nevertheless, while religions are many, truth is one; and all religions cannot be one, given their differing truth claims about the ultimate reality, humanity, morality, spiritual liberation, the afterlife, and more.[9] There are many approaches or methods to the study of religion, but mine is self-consciously cognitive and apologetic. I address the central *doctrines* of each religion (1) in relation to Christianity (to show similarities and differences) and (2) attempt to ascertain how each religion testifies before the bar

---

[7]Robert Louis Wilken, *Liberty in the Things of God: The Christian Origins of Religious Freedom* (New Haven, CT: Yale University Press, 2019).

[8]A popular book, now in its sixth edition, takes up this issue. See Stewart M. Matlins and Arthur J. Magida, eds., *How to Be a Perfect Stranger: The Essential Religious Etiquette Handbook*, 6th ed. (Nashville: SkyLight Paths, 2015).

[9]See Mortimer J. Adler, *Truth in Religion: The Plurality of Religions and the Unity of Truth* (New York: Touchstone, 1992); and Stephen Prothero, *God Is Not One: Eight Rival Religions That Run the World* (New York: HarperOne, 2011).

of truth. You should not be surprised, then, to find my evaluations of each faith after discussing their central tenets. My conviction is that truth is found in the gospel of Jesus Christ, so it will serve as the lens through which I understand other faiths and other claims to the truth. But our first sentence concerns the rejection of all religion and of any sacred aspect of reality. It was uttered by the son of a Lutheran pastor, Friedrich Nietzsche. If Nietzsche is correct, then *false* could be written over all the subsequent six sentences. To him we now turn.

one

ATHEISM

1

"God is dead."

All religion is defeated and refuted if it can be shown that there is no God and no sacred reality. Monotheism affirms that there is one transcendent and personal God who created the world and who deserves worship and obedience on his terms. Other religions demur but affirm a sacred reality that is irreducible to any material state, such as the Buddhist idea of Nirvana, the Hindu concept of Brahman, or the Daoist concept of the Dao. We will evaluate these claims shortly, but our attention is first drawn to the pronouncement of a famous eighteenth-century German atheist, a man who stripped the cosmos of God or any sacred reality or purpose. So opposed was he to Christianity that he penned a book called *The Anti-Christ* to make it clear. If he is right, all religions are wrong, and we must make our way alone in an uncaring and godless cosmos.

NIETZSCHE'S WORLD WITHOUT GOD

Friedrich Nietzsche (1844–1900) was a passionate writer whose literary brilliance and sweeping philosophical judgments have left a deep and wide mark on philosophy and beyond. Walter Kaufmann, who translated and edited *The Portable Nietzsche*, writes of Nietzsche's "brilliant epigrams and metaphors, his sparkling polemics and ceaseless stylistic experiments."[1] As a freshman in college, I was dazzled by both the style and the philosophy for a time, and carried around my *Portable Nietzsche* like an atheist Bible.[2]

Having received his doctorate without needing to write a dissertation, Nietzsche quickly gained status academically as a philologist and a philosopher.[3] However, bad health caused him to leave the classroom, and he spent the rest of his life on a pension as an intellectual nomad, traveling through Europe, looking for healthy climes, and writing his iconoclastic books while chronically ill.

Nietzsche is most known for a bold three-word statement and for a sad twelve-year condition. The condition is insanity, which overtook him in 1884, thus ending his writing. After seeing a horse being beaten on the street, the great advocate of the hypermasculine overman threw his arms around the beast and fell into insanity. His statement, *God is dead*, was made in his right mind and with a flourish as part of a parable called "The Madman," from *The Gay Science*. It must be quoted in full, given the drama and craft of it.

---

[1]Friedrich Nietzsche, *The Portable Nietzsche*, ed. and trans. Walter Kaufmann, Portable Library (New York: Viking Penguin, 1982), 1, Kindle.

[2]Consider the old line, "If your Bible is falling apart (from use), then your life probably isn't." Applied to Nietzsche, "If your *Portable Nietzsche* is falling apart," your life probably is too.

[3]This was no administrative oversight. It was Germany, after all. His supervisors deemed him so brilliant that a dissertation would be superfluous. In contrast, I wrote two dissertations for my doctorate in philosophy since the first was rejected.

Have you not heard of that madman who lit a lantern in the bright morning hours, ran to the market place, and cried incessantly, "I seek God! I seek God!" As many of those who do not believe in God were standing around just then, he provoked much laughter. Why, did he get lost? said one. Did he lose his way like a child? said another. Or is he hiding? Is he afraid of us? Has he gone on a voyage? or emigrated? Thus they yelled and laughed. The madman jumped into their midst and pierced them with his glances.

"Whither is God" he cried. "I shall tell you. We have killed him—you and I. All of us are his murderers. But how have we done this? How were we able to drink up the sea? Who gave us the sponge to wipe away the entire horizon? What did we do when we unchained this earth from its sun? Whither is it moving now? Whither are we moving now? Away from all suns? Are we not plunging continually? Backward, sideward, forward, in all directions? Is there any up or down left? Are we not straying as through an infinite nothing? Do we not feel the breath of empty space? Has it not become colder? Is not night and more night coming on all the while? Must not lanterns be lit in the morning? Do we not hear anything yet of the noise of the gravediggers who are burying God? Do we not smell anything yet of God's decomposition? Gods too decompose. God is dead. God remains dead. And we have killed him. How shall we, the murderers of all murderers, comfort ourselves? What was holiest and most powerful of all that the world has yet owned has bled to death under our knives. Who will wipe this blood off us? What water is there for us to clean ourselves? What festivals of atonement, what sacred games shall we have to invent? Is not the greatness of this deed too great for us? Must not we ourselves become gods simply to seem worthy of it? There has never been a greater deed; and whoever will be born after us—for the sake of this deed he will be part of a higher history than all history hitherto."

Here the madman fell silent and looked again at his listeners; and they too were silent and stared at him in astonishment. At last he threw his lantern on the ground, and it broke and went out. "I come too early," he said then; "my time has not come yet. This tremendous event is still on its way, still wandering—it has not yet reached the ears of man. Lightning and thunder require time, the light of the stars requires time, deeds require time even after they are done, before they can be seen and heard. This deed is still more distant from them than the most distant stars—and yet they have done it themselves."

It has been related further that on that same day the madman entered divers churches and there sang his *requiem aeternam deo*. Led out and called to account, he is said to have replied each time, "What are these churches now if they are not the tombs and sepulchers of God?"[4]

This episode, taken from *The Gay Science*, gives no arguments against the existence of God, although we will address three of them below. Rather, it assumes the nonexistence of God and poetically and dramatically draws out the personal and social implications of atheism. *God is dead* means that (1) there is no God and never has been; (2) the belief in God's nonexistence has dire and dramatic implications for culture, politics, history, and religion; and (3) these world-historical implications will inevitably be worked out over time, thus changing everything in human affairs where Christianity has held sway.

---

[4]Nietzsche, *Portable Nietzsche*, 95-96.

This parable can be read as a prediction or as a warning or as both. It is a warning in two senses. First, to Nietzsche's sense. His image of an earth unchained from the sun and spinning without purpose in space was a world stripped of deity and of every belief that God requires the existence of God to be true. Earth shorn of God makes a person an ersatz god, the god who murdered God. Nietzsche wonders what kind of "atonement" is required of such an act, indicating guilt and the need for redemption. But there is no such atonement. Atheistic executioners must face the severity of their act because a world without God does not remain the same, except that religion ceases to have an object. Rather, every value that required God as its root is uprooted, and what remains is a godless landscape lacking any map or compass or guide. Thus, Nietzsche called for the "revaluation of all values."[5]

Nietzsche demanded that God's murderers accept their plight with realism. Only a few brave men (and he meant males) would have the courage to forge their own values, deny any heaven of ideas or divine revelation, and assert their "will-to-power" over lesser folks. Nietzsche's character, Zarathustra, a kind of prophet without God, thunders forth:

> Verily, men gave themselves all their good and evil. Verily, they did not take it, they did not find it, nor did it come to them as a voice from heaven. Only man placed values in things to preserve himself—he alone created a meaning for things, a human meaning. Therefore he calls himself "man," which means: the esteemer.[6]

When heaven is emptied of God, history will change radically. Any sense of providence, human rights, the priority of love, or

---

[5]Kauffman uses the word *revaluation*. See Nietzsche, *Portable Nietzsche*, 568-69. This is the preface to Friedrich Nietzsche, *The Anti-Christ*, originally published in 1895.
[6]Nietzsche, *Portable Nietzsche*, 171.

divine judgment vanishes. It would take time, but it would happen. The nerve for altruism would be severed. Only the select few could hear and heed these words of Nietzsche, the atheist prophet.

To esteem is to create: hear this, you creators! Esteeming itself is of all esteemed things the most estimable treasure. Through esteeming alone is there value: and without esteeming, the nut of existence would be hollow. Hear this, you creators![7]

What, if anything, could give meaning in Nietzsche's world without God? Since "the nut of existence" is hollow in itself, all meaning stems from individuals, although few would have the courage to own it. Most would either pretend that atheism had no severe consequences or live by using religion as a crutch to compensate for their weakness. As an undergraduate, I attended a lecture by a historian who made an offhanded remark that although he did not believe in God, he still held most of the moral values of a religious person. He said this flippantly, and many laughed. I did not. Nietzsche would not have laughed either. That man had cheated philosophically.

The path to meaning, for Nietzsche, brings us to the doorstep of the overman. As he said in *Thus Spoke Zarathustra*, "Man is a rope, tied between beast and overman—a rope over an abyss."[8] Humans were not made in the image of God, as the Bible teaches, he argues, yet humans could be more than mere animals. "Overman" is Walter Kaufmann's translation of *Übermensch*, a crucial idea for Nietzsche. The overman strives to overcome whatever would overshadow his own individuality and originality as a unique and incomparable creator of value. As Kaufmann puts it, the overman is

---

[7]Nietzsche, *Portable Nietzsche*, 171.
[8]Nietzsche, *Portable Nietzsche*, 126.

a human being who has created for himself that unique position in the cosmos which the Bible considered his divine birthright. The meaning of life is thus found on earth, in this life, not as the inevitable outcome of evolution . . . but in the few human beings who raise themselves above the all-too-human mass.[9]

As Zarathustra intones six times, "Man is something that must be overcome."[10] By "man," Nietzsche means human beings understood as having a fixed and given human nature and as accountable to God. To that he says good riddance, and longs for overman. Rudolf Steiner (1861–1925) noted that Nietzsche did not find meaning in the newly developed scientific idea of evolution, which guaranteed no human excellence, only change. Nietzsche

asked himself how he could live with the new idea [of evolution]. His battle took place entirely within his own soul. He needed the further development to the superman [or overman] in order to be able to bear mankind.[11]

Thus, in order to find meaning, humans without God have to aspire to be more than humans but less than God—and to so endeavor while walking a tightrope strung over an abyss. "The overman is the meaning of the earth. Let your will say: the overman shall be the meaning of the earth!"[12] Nietzsche often uses repetition and exclamation marks to do philosophical work since he vouchsafes little about just what an overman is. Whatever he is, he is not the result of mere evolutionary change. Optimistic humanism was not an option for Nietzsche since it

---

[9]Nietzsche, *Portable Nietzsche*, 115-16.
[10]Nietzsche, *Portable Nietzsche*, 149.
[11]Rudolf Steiner, *Friedrich Nietzsche: Fighter for Freedom* (Englewood, NJ: Steiner, 1960), 211.
[12]Nietzsche, *Portable Nietzsche*, 125.

cannot appeal to any good human potential, since human nature has to be overcome. And, of course, there is no transcendent standard or ideal. The overman seems stranded in a meaningless universe from which no meaning can be sculpted.

A second source of potential meaning for Nietzsche is "the eternal recurrence," or the idea that everything that has happened will happen again, ad infinitum. This is not the biblical idea of eternal life—an unending and blessed afterlife in a linear series. Rather, it is a cyclical view—life in this world as it is, over and over again. As he puts it, the "eternal hourglass of existence is turned over and over, and you with it, a dust grain of dust."[13] He asks "how well disposed would you have to become to yourself and to life to crave nothing more fervently than this ultimate eternal confirmation and seal?"[14] Some debate whether Nietzsche took this to be objectively true of the cosmos or instead as a poetic mode of embracing life.[15] Either way, the idea fails to confer any purpose for life or death. The repetition of zero is still zero, even if zero is multiplied by infinity.

Nietzsche's Case Against Religion

Nietzsche trained the heavy artillery of his philosophical objections against the religions of Judaism and Christianity specifically since they influenced Germany and the Western world more than other religions. He had some appreciation of Buddhism but not its essential worldview, which includes metaphysical elements—such as reincarnation, karma, and

---

[13]Nietzsche, *Portable Nietzsche*, 101.

[14]Nietzsche, *Portable Nietzsche*, 102.

[15]The "scientific argument" is that if the universe is eternal in time but finite in scope, then everything will recycle endlessly. However, scientific and philosophical evidence refutes the notion of an eternal universe. See Douglas Groothuis, *Christian Apologetics: A Comprehensive Case for Biblical Faith*, 2nd ed. (Downers Grove, IL: IVP Academic, 2022).

Nirvana—that his materialistic atheism disallowed. He preferred the Buddhist view of suffering to that of Christianity:

> Buddhism, I repeat, a hundred times colder, more truthful, more objective [than Christianity]. It is no longer confronted with the need to make suffering and the susceptibility to pain respectable by interpreting them in terms of sin—it simply says what it thinks: "I suffer."[16]

Nietzsche did not subject Buddhism to the severe criticism he reserved for Judaism and especially Christianity. Let us address his case against biblical religion.

First, Nietzsche defied God more than he denied God's existence. He was not able to bear the idea that God knew everything about him. "The god who saw everything, even man—this god had to die! Man cannot bear it that such a witness should live."[17] Again:

> That we find no God—either in history or in nature or behind nature—is not what differentiates us, but that we experience what has been revered as God, not as "godlike" but as miserable, as absurd, as harmful, not merely as an error but *as a crime against life*. We deny God as God. If one were to prove this God of the Christians to us, we should be even less able to believe in him.[18]

Nietzsche's critique is that the Christian God is antilife and untrue to the earth, which is our only reality. "I beseech you, my brothers, remain faithful to the earth, and do not believe those who speak to you of otherworldly hopes! Poison-mixers are they, whether they know it or not."[19]

---

[16]Nietzsche, *Portable Nietzsche*, 590.
[17]Nietzsche, *Portable Nietzsche*, 379.
[18]Nietzsche, *Portable Nietzsche*, 627.
[19]Nietzsche, *Portable Nietzsche*, 125.

For his critique to stand, Nietzsche must find value in the naked earth *sans deo* [without God]. But this, as I have argued, is unavailable to him since all value is asserted by individuals whose intrinsic value is null and void, since the earth has been unchained from the sun and is spinning aimlessly through empty space.

Further, his critique of Christianity as antilife is false.[20] According to Christianity, God created the world as "very good" and made humans in his image and likeness (Gen 1). But given the fall, some aspects of life—sinful thoughts and behaviors—need to be denied in order to affirm higher aspects of life, faith, and virtue. Jesus' atoning suffering and death wrought the forgiveness of sin, but it did not deny the essential goodness of life for those who follow him. As he promised,

> I am the gate; whoever enters through me will be saved. They will come in and go out, and find pasture. The thief comes only to steal and kill and destroy; I have come that they may have life, and have it to the full. (Jn 10:9-10)

The apostle Paul concurs, "God . . . richly provides us with everything for our enjoyment" (1 Tim 6:17). Ecclesiastes repeatedly commends the enjoyment of life given by God, despite the ephemerality and disappointments of a world east of Eden and "under the sun" (Eccl 2:24-25; 5:18-20). Further, the Song of Songs celebrates the joys of erotic love between husband and wife.[21]

Nietzsche's second attack on biblical religion is that it breeds *ressentiment*, a French word meaning "a feeling of bitter anger

---

[20]For a more detailed argument, see Douglas Groothuis, "Nietzsche's Evaluation of Christian Ethics" (1986), http://library.mibckerala.org/lms_frame/eBook/TI1/Evaluation%20of%20Christian%20Ethics.pdf.

[21]See S. Craig Glickman, *A Song for Lovers* (Downers Grove, IL: InterVarsity Press, 1976).

or resentment together with a sense of frustration at being pow-
erless to express this hostility."[22] For Nietzsche, Judaism
was a slave religion and Christianity continued the grievance.
Ressentiment is wielded by the losers in history against the
winners, whom they condemn as immoral as a way to recom-
pense their own lack of power. It is "slave morality," not "master
morality," that thrives on the exercise of power. So, for Nietzsche,
Jesus' statement that "the meek will inherit the earth" (Mt 5:5)
really means that the weak desire to depose the strong through
the alien power of God (who does not exist). To cite Frank Zappa
in a Nietzschean tone, "The meek shall inherit nothing."[23] Or as
a graffito I once saw put it, "The earth inherits the meek."

However, this critique only holds if there is no God whose
judgments are true and whose ways are trustworthy. Nietzsche
has not shown that. If there is no such deity, then the losers of
history might well rely on *ressentiment* to compensate for their
impotence. But even so, Nietzsche's judgment about Christian
morality and psychology is off base since Christianity teaches us
to love and pray for our enemies (Mt 5:43-48) and offers salvation to all who will humble themselves before God and have
faith in Christ as Savior (Eph 2:8). Both the high and the low will
stand before the infallible and inevitable judgment of God.
Moreover, not a few biblical characters are strong and presti-
gious socially, such as David and Solomon. Saul, who became
the apostle Paul, was a high achiever intellectually and religiously before his conversion, and he did not cease to demon-
strate his intellect afterward (see especially Acts 17:16-34).[24]

---

[22]*Collins English Dictionary*, s.v. "ressentiment (n.)," (in American English), accessed Feb-
ruary 24, 2023, www.collinsdictionary.com/dictionary/english/ressentiment.

[23]Frank Zappa, "The Meek Will Inherit Nothing," Zappa Family Trust, 1981.

[24]See Douglas Groothuis, "Learning from an Apostle," *Christian Research Journal* (July 1,
2019), www.equip.org/articles/learning-from-an-apostle-christianity-in-the-marketplace
-of-ideas-acts-1716-34.

There is no sign of *ressentiment* in his actions or teachings. However, in light of knowing Christ, he counted this all as nothing, as is proper if the goodness of eternal life outweighs all earthy achievements (Phil 3:8).

Nietzsche launched a third attack against God:

> A god who is all-knowing and all-powerful and who does not even make sure that his creatures understand his intention—could that be a god of goodness? Who allows countless doubts and dubieties to persist, for thousands of years, as though the salvation of mankind were unaffected by them, and who on the other hand holds out the prospect of frightful consequences if any mistake is made as to the nature of truth?[25]

Thus, this God is like "a deaf and dumb man making all kinds of ambiguous signs when the most fearful danger is about to fall on his child or his dog."[26] This objection is now called "the hiddenness of God." If God is who monotheism claims, why then do not more people believe in him? So, it would seem, the claim that (1) God exists and (2) many do not believe in God are incompatible.

I address this elsewhere in some detail,[27] but the heart of the matter is the matter of the human heart and God's manner of communicating. People may or may not respond wisely to the evidence God sets before them. They are intellectual agents who make cognitive choices based on their values. This is why Jesus said, "Whoever has ears, let them hear" (Mt 13:9). As Pascal wrote, "There is enough light for those who desire only to see,

---

[25]Friedrich Nietzsche, *Daybreak: Thoughts on the Prejudices of Morality*, trans. R. J. Hollingdale (Cambridge: Cambridge University Press, 1985), 52.

[26]Nietzsche, *Daybreak*, 53.

[27]Groothuis, "Doubt, Skepticism, and the Hiddenness of God," in *Christian Apologetics*.

and enough darkness for those of a contrary disposition."[28] We can conclude, thus:

1. There is ample evidence for God's existence from natural theology.[29]
2. God exists.
3. But many do not believe in God.
4. Proposition (3) is explained by our cognitive freedom. Some are disposed not to believe, even though there is strong evidence for God's existence.
5. Therefore (3) gives no evidence that (2) is false.

Nietzsche's disposition was obvious, and his anti-God arguments were specious.

NIETZSCHE'S GRIM LESSON

Nietzsche's atheism was ill-founded, but his predictions about a world where the divine horizon is wiped out have proven grimly true. Religion, in all its forms, affirms a transcendent source of morality, while Nietzsche denied it. As C. S. Lewis wrote, in "Platonic, Aristotelian, Stoic, Christian, and Oriental" thought alike is "the doctrine of objective value, the belief that certain attitudes are really true, and others really false, to the kind of thing the universe is and the kind of things we are."[30] In *The Abolition of Man*, Lewis called this reality "the Tao" in a religiously neutral sense. We will later explore whether the nontheistic "Oriental" understandings of objective moral value are up for the metaphysical task. Without this "doctrine of objective value," nihilism and totalitarianism beckon since everything loses all intrinsic and objective value grounded in any transcendent standard.

---

[28]Blaise Pascal, *Pensées*, trans. A. J. Krailsheimer (New York: Penguin, 1966), 149 (item 430), 50.

[29]See Groothuis, "The Case for Christian Theism," in *Christian Apologetics*.

[30]C. S. Lewis, *The Abolition of Man* (New York: HarperOne, 2001), 19, Kindle.

Nietzsche accused Christianity as leading to nihilism because of its antilife stance. He thought it emptied the earth of meaning because of a nonexistent heaven. He was wrong. Nietzsche thought he could avoid nihilism through the aspiration to the overman. He was wrong again, since overman does not exist—except in the mind of Friedrich Nietzsche. He was right about the effects of atheism, however. Atheism is the high-octane fuel of totalitarianism since political power reigns free of the fear of God.

Nietzsche was no socialist since socialism's ideal is to level society and create equality. That would justify the "herd mentality" of lesser wills and lesser lights that he despised. However, the philosophical and political titan of socialism of the twentieth century was atheistic—Marxism. Marxism left approximately one hundred million killed by their own totalitarian, Marxist-atheist governments in China, the USSR, Cambodia, and elsewhere.[31] Marxism substituted a secular and economic sense of purpose to history in which the poor rise up to overcome the rich and promote an egalitarian society. This has never happened anywhere, and Marx never gave a sufficient justification why anyone would expect this to happen through political means. But wherever Marxism has been tried, it has denied intrinsic human rights, treated people as the means to political ends even at the cost of their lives, and prevented freedom of speech and freedom of religion—since there was no God to give these rights. It likewise worked to overturn the traditional family in order to make the state the supreme social entity. This carnage and political repression are attributable to atheism on a grand scale. Nietzsche was right about that.

---

[31]See Stéphane Courtois et al., *The Black Book of Communism: Crimes, Terror, Repression*, trans. Jonathan Murphy and Mark Kramer (Cambridge, MA: Harvard University Press, 1999).

While atheism is not a sufficient condition for massive injustice on a revolutionary scale, it is a necessary condition for it, and makes it more likely.[32] Since Nietzsche defended atheism, he made totalitarianism more likely. As Russian dissident Alexandr Solzhenitsyn said:

> It was Dostoevsky, once again, who drew from the French Revolution and its seeming hatred of the Church the lesson that "revolution must necessarily begin with atheism." That is absolutely true. But the world had never before known a godlessness as organized, militarized, and tenaciously malevolent as that practiced by Marxism. Within the philosophical system of Marx and Lenin, and at the heart of their psychology, hatred of God is the principal driving force, more fundamental than all their political and economic pretensions. Militant atheism is not merely incidental or marginal to Communist policy; it is not a side effect, but the central pivot to achieve its diabolical ends. Communism needs to control a population devoid of religious and national feeling, and this entails the destruction of faith and nationhood. Communists proclaim both of these objectives openly, and just as openly go about carrying them out.[33]

What was true of the USSR was (and is) true of communist China, which enforces atheism and persecutes religious believers of all kinds. The totalitarian state can brook no religious rivals.

My point is not that Nietzsche advocated anything like Marxism. He did not. However, a world without God is ripe for

---

[32]While religion has been advanced to oppress and murder others, it cannot match the murderous results of the twentieth century atheism in this respect.

[33]Alexandr Solzhenitsyn, "'Men Have Forgotten God': Aleksandr Solzhenitsyn's 1983 Templeton Address," *National Review*, December 11, 2018, www.nationalreview .com/2018/12/aleksandr-solzhenitsyn-men-have-forgotten-god-speech.

ersatz gods, as Nietzsche said, and some of these will take as their kingdom the most ruthless political oppression. Nietzsche revered Napoleon for his aristocratic nature and exceptional will-to-power, calling him a "synthesis of the inhuman and the superhuman."[34] He valorized men of great strength who were not restrained by love or by a religious conscience. For them, there was no God to fear or worship, but there was a world to win through power and even cruelty. It is no surprise that Adolf Hitler drew inspiration from Nietzsche—whether or not Nietzsche was antisemitic.[35]

While some atheists have tried to go on as if little changes with the death of God—since we can supposedly support objective moral values apart from God—Nietzsche had no such illusions. Before giving a long list of excoriations against Christianity, Nietzsche affirms, "In Christianity neither morality nor religion has even a single point of contact with reality."[36] Further:

> When one gives up the Christian faith, one pulls the right
> to Christian morality out from under one's feet. This mo-
> rality is by no means self-evident. . . . Christianity is a
> system, a whole view of things thought out together. By
> breaking one main concept out of it, the faith in God, one
> breaks the whole: nothing necessary remains in one's
> hands. Christianity presupposes that man does not know,
> cannot know, what is good for him, what is evil: he believes
> in God, who alone knows it. Christian morality is a
> command; its origin is transcendent; it is beyond all

---

[34]Friedrich Nietzsche, *On the Genealogy of Morals*, ed. Douglas Smith, Oxford World's Classics (Oxford: Oxford University Press, 2008), 35-37, Kindle.
[35]Stephen R. C. Hicks, *Nietzsche and the Nazis: A Personal View* (Roscoe, IL: Ockham's Razor Press, 2010).
[36]Nietzsche, *Portable Nietzsche*, 581.

criticism, all right to criticism; it has truth only if God is the truth—it stands and falls with faith in God.[37]

There is no way to rescue the traditional classical or Judeo-Christian virtues or civil society in the atheistic world of Nietzsche. The "revaluation of values" leaves nothing at it was.

ATHEISM, MORAL MEANING, AND RELIGION

Along with Nietzsche, atheists such as Max Stirner, Jean-Paul Sartre, Albert Camus, Michael Ruse, and others have claimed that God is the only possible source of objective morality and meaning. Without God, we must find another way. Other atheists try to retain objective morality in a godless and directionless world, although their case is weak.[38] Nietzsche shows us that without God traditional concepts of meaning and morality crumble. But neither his reasons for disbelieving in God nor his godless moral alternative is compelling. Here is the essential argument of this chapter.

1. Without God or some sacred realm, there can be no "objective moral value" (C. S. Lewis). Nietzsche agrees.
2. Nietzsche's reasons for atheism fail.
3. Nietzsche's godless alternative to objective moral value (the overman) fails to give meaning.
4. Nietzsche's case against God fails.
5. Without objective moral value or Nietzsche's (or some other) alternative, we face nihilism.
6. Nihilism easily leads to totalitarianism (and other evils).
7. Totalitarianism is evil and has led to mass slaughter in the twentieth century.

---

[37]Nietzsche, *Portable Nietzsche*, 515-16.
[38]Groothuis, "The Moral Argument for God," in *Christian Apologetics*.

8. Therefore, to avoid evil, we need to posit God or some sacred realm to ground objective moral value and to curb totalitarianism (and other evils).

We will consider the worldviews of the major world religions through the prisms of each religion's representative sentence. At this point in the argument, we have learned that atheism (Nietzsche's or otherwise) cannot ground the morally meaningful life that we desire. It remains to be seen which of the major world religions can rise to this philosophical occasion. We begin with Judaism's statement, *I am who I am.*

- two -

JUDAISM

"I am who I am."

2

Our parents give us our names, and we give our children their names, usually after considerable deliberation. We name our pets too. Some names are chosen because of their sound; some of us are named after family members, others because of their meaning. Parents who name a girl Hope likely hope she will be a woman of hope. The same goes for Faith and other virtue names. We may later change our names, but this is a second thought. We come into the world as named by another. Names can be blessings, or names can be curses. Several times in the Bible God renamed people in light of their calling. Abram becomes Abraham, for example (Gen 17:1-6). But the God of the Jews was named not by another but by himself (Ex 3:15). John Piper explains the significance:

> And when he names himself, we may be sure the name is packed with who he is and what he intends to do. God does not choose names for himself at random, say for the sound

or for an ancestor or to avoid embarrassing nicknames. He chooses names for the sake of revealing things about himself that will deepen our love for him and enlarge our admiration and strengthen our faith.[1]

While the God of the Hebrew Bible has many names, one uniquely—if a bit mysteriously—captures the essence of his superlative being. Because of that name, a nation is formed and understood, a worldview is discerned, a religion is founded, and our world has been transformed. It appears in a story, as do most things in the Hebrew Bible. We must abbreviate this story here.

Moses came in the line of people chosen by God, starting with Abram, to make God known to the nations and to bless them by divine covenant. While God's people were under Egyptian bondage, God favored Moses by saving him as an infant and by placing him in Pharoah's household. After Moses' abortive attempt to take justice into his own hands by killing an Egyptian, followed by a long exile, something strange happened. Consider a fire, a voice, a two-way conversation, and a name.

While Moses was tending a flock at Mount Horeb, he saw a burning bush that was not consumed by the flames. He heard a voice call his name and claim that he had heard the cries of Moses' people for deliverance (Ex 3). These words may be familiar to us, but remember they were spoken by a voice in a fire in a bush that was not consumed by flames. After God declared his intensions to free the Jews through Moses, Moses needed more information. He dared to ask a question in this bizarre but compelling situation.

Moses said to God, "Suppose I go to the Israelites and say to them, 'The God of your fathers has sent me to you,'

---

[1]John Piper, "I Am Who I Am" (Ex 3:15-17), sermon, Bethlehem Baptist Church, Minneapolis, MN, September 16, 1984, www.desiringgod.org/messages/i-am-who-i-am.

and they ask me, 'What is his name?' Then what shall I
tell them?"

God said to Moses, "I AM WHO I AM. This is what you
are to say to the Israelites: 'I AM has sent me to you.'"
(Ex 3:13-14)

Before exploring the meaning of *I am who I am*, the communicative situation needs to be explained by several categories.

First, God initiates a *rational* conversation with Moses by
calling *his* name. However extraordinary or supernatural the
burning bush was, God spoke to Moses in discernible language
that Moses could understand and to which he could respond in
his own words. Jews and Christians may take this for granted,
but they should not, given its significance. When we consider
Hinduism, Buddhism, and Daoism, we find that the ultimate
reality is not a person who speaks truth but an ineffable (that is,
wordless) dimension that can supposedly be experienced
through enlightenment, which is an altered state of consciousness. Not so for Moses, who simply heard his name called;
observed a strange, but identifiable, phenomenon (the burning
bush); and listened to that voice, which spoke in a language he
understood. It was completely rational and completely supernatural. Communication is rational when it states intelligible
content without contradiction. (*Rational* here does not necessarily mean giving a logical argument but is used to describe
statements as intelligible, discernible, or comprehensible.)

Neither the laws of logic nor the essential principles of human
communication (proper grammar, syntax, and vocabulary)
were suspended or transcended in this event; it was spectacular
but not irrational. Put another way, this communication was
rational and verbal. Since it was communication from God to a
man (and later to many more through its inscripturation in the

Bible), it was a divine *revelation*. If it was a revelation or dis-closure from God, then it is objectively true and trustworthy. What God says can be believed rationally and, thus, may be taken as knowledge. In fact, God claims that what he says will be confirmed by events.

Since the word *revelation* can mean many things, we need to continue to investigate this story of Moses and God to mine its treasures. Carl F. H. Henry put well the biblical idea of reve-lation: "Revelation in the Bible is essentially a mental conception: God's disclosure is rational and intelligible communication. Is-suing from the mind and will of God, revelation is addressed to the mind and will of human beings."[2]

Divine revelation may involve historical particularities (a burning bush) and various sensory events or visions; it may arouse strong feeling or no feelings; it may be intellectually simple or more complex; it may be written in various languages (Saul heard Jesus speak in to him in Aramaic [Acts 26:14]); it may be symbolic or literal; it may be understood or misunderstood. But for revelation to be revelation at all, it must be "rational and intelligible communication" from God's mind to our minds. That is, there must be *propositional content*.

Propositions have gotten a bad name in some circles—especially among some Christian theologians—but they are in-dispensable for knowledge, whether from God or from human beings. A proposition is what a statement asserts. The same proposition, "God exists," can be stated in English, French, Arabic, or in any language. The languages differ, but their meaning does not. The unity of meaning is only explicable on the basis of propositions.

---

[2]Carl F. H. Henry, *God, Revelation and Authority*, vol. 3 (Wheaton, IL: Crossway, 1999), 248, Kindle.

Verbal assertions—written, spoken, or thought—require propositions. "God exists" is a proposition. "God does not exist" is a proposition. On the other hand, a question (or an interrogative) requests information and is not a proposition proper. Moses' following statement is a question, "Suppose I go to the Israelites and say to them, 'The God of your fathers has sent me to you,' and they ask me, 'What is his name?' Then what shall I tell them?" God's response is a proposition: "This is what you are to say to the Israelites: 'I AM has sent me to you.'" Besides this, there are imperative statements, such as when God warns Moses in the account we are discussing, "'Do not come any closer,' God said. 'Take off your sandals, for the place where you are standing is holy ground'" (Ex 3:5).

There is propositional content for questions and imperatives as well. Moses asks for information (propositions) from God. Affirming that "Moses asked for information from God," is a way of propositionalizing this question. The same can be said for commands: "God told Moses to take off his sandals."

I have belabored philosophical concepts on rationality and propositions because they are necessary to grasp the existential and historical significance of God's name as revealed to Moses. If the Jewish understanding of God's name and nature had been relegated to a murky, mystical experience or to a merely cultural function, Judaism as we know it would never have existed. Nor would have Christianity existed after it, since it builds on the notion of revelation.

While God's name, *I am who I am*, is written out in the Hebrew Bible, Jews have historically been reluctant to speak the actual Hebrew name, given its holiness. As Jewish philosopher Abraham Heschel noted, "Throughout the ages the Jews shrank from uttering, and, to some degree, even from writing out in full the four-lettered Holy Name of God (the Tetragrammaton).

Except in the Bible, the name is usually not written out in full."[3] Some observant Jews will not spell out God, but use G-d. This name is YHWH (the Tetragrammaton) and may be pronounced as Yahweh (as it is spelled in English). YHWH is the Hebrew word behind the word LORD (all capital letters) in English Bibles. It is the most important name for God in the Hebrew Bible and is used 6,828 times.[4]

Jews believe the name was revealed by God. While we have inherited the notion that revelation and rationality are opposed to one another, this idea is alien to the Hebrew Bible (and the New Testament as well). How this false dichotomy occurred is a long and vexed story, but Yoram Hazony argues that this dichotomy is absent from the Hebrew Scriptures, which offer a robust philosophy of life with God at the center.[5] This God speaks and shows himself through revelation and history. But what exactly does this name mean?

I am who I am sounds like a tautology (A is A). Everyone is who they are. Everything is what it is. Or we can take it as stating the law of identity: something is identical to itself and not something different. Or think of the refrain made when something cannot be changed: "It is what it is." But *I am who I am* is far different from all of that.

Since God is speaking in cognizable words, he is a *personal being*, not an impersonal or abstract force or principle. He is not the impersonal divine substance of the Stoics or the impersonal absolute identity of the Hindu Brahman or the Dao "that cannot be spoken" of in Daoism. The Buddhist Nirvana does not speak,

[3]Abraham Joshua Heschel, *God in Search of Man* (New York: Farrar, Straus and Giroux, 1955), 64, Kindle.
[4]Piper, "I Am Who I Am."
[5]Yoram Hazony, *The Philosophy of Hebrew Scripture* (New York: Cambridge University Press, 2012).

nor does the Buddha, beyond what he spoke on earth, since he no longer exists as a personal being.[6] Put another way, God is a Self, a center of consciousness, who has the ability to think, feel, speak, act, and make himself known in words and deeds. God is "I am," not "It is." God is a *who*, not a *what*. The "I am" is spoken by itself. The "It is" is not spoken and cannot be spoken by itself since it is mute in principle.

Our association with human persons—who can say, "I am"— is of a different order than our association with things although we can, to our shame, treat persons as things or objects. We experience things, but they do not experience us. However, through deep listening and empathy, we can experience a communion with other people in which each person encounters the other as a conscious being of unique worth and depth. A singular aspect of a person is the ability or potential to communicate from his or her reflective consciousness. According to our text, God, as a personal being, has the ability to hear as well as speak. Moreover, he makes promises and predictions that the promises will prove true. It is the voice of authority for individuals, a nation, the nations, history, and beyond.

The answer *I am who I am* is utterly unlike the answers we receive from human beings. If someone asks you, "Who are you?," would you say, "I am who I am"? You would rather likely tell the person your given name (which you did not give yourself, unless you changed your name), and you might further mention other contingent facts about yourself, such as your profession or marital status. But God's answer is only about himself—in and through and of and by himself. There is nothing beyond or behind God through which to explain him. And thus God is

---

[6]Buddhists claim that Buddha entered Nirvana at death, but this is nothing like the Jewish, Christian, or Islamic view of the afterlife since Nirvana means extinguishment and the end of personality.

self-existent, depending on nothing outside of himself for this existence or character.[7]

Just before God revealed his name to Moses, he made this promise based on his evaluation and concern. Abraham Heschel wrote of the "divine pathos" made known through the prophets.[8] We find compassion in the following passage in which God speaks.

> "I have indeed seen the misery of my people in Egypt. I have heard them crying out because of their slave drivers, and I am concerned about their suffering. So I have come down to rescue them from the hand of the Egyptians and to bring them up out of that land into a good and spacious land, a land flowing with milk and honey—the home of the Canaanites, Hittites, Amorites, Perizzites, Hivites and Jebusites. And now the cry of the Israelites has reached me, and I have seen the way the Egyptians are oppressing them. So now, go. I am sending you to Pharaoh to bring my people the Israelites out of Egypt." (Ex 3:7-10)

God fulfilled his promise. He delivered his people from Egypt and brought them into the Promised Land. These acts are rooted in the name and nature of God as "I am." An alternative translation for God's disclosure of his name is "I will be who I will be." This indicates God's unchanging faithfulness. As he said in Israel's story, through the prophet Malachi, "I the LORD do not change. So you, the descendants of Jacob, are not destroyed" (Mal 3:6). So, too, the psalmist cries out:

> In the beginning you laid the foundations of the earth,
>   and the heavens are the work of your hands.

---

[7]The apostle Paul also affirms this in Acts 17:25.

[8]Abraham Joshua Heschel, "The Divine Pathos," in *The Prophets*, 2 vols. in 1 (orig. pub. 1962; Peabody, MA: Hendrickson Academic, 2007).

They will perish, but you remain;
    they will all wear out like a garment.
Like clothing you will change them
    and they will be discarded.
But you remain the same,
    and your years will never end. (Ps 102:25-27)[9]

Because God is complete in himself and does not change, his promised actions in history come true. *I am who I am* is not of two minds; neither is he unable to save and establish his ways in the world. He is faithful to his word since his word is based on his name. As the prophet later proclaims,

The LORD is the everlasting God,
    the Creator of the ends of the earth.
He will not grow tired or weary,
    and his understanding no one can fathom. (Is 40:28)

THE STORY CONTINUES

God's revelation of himself as *I am who I am* was not the beginning of the Jewish story by any means. That can be traced to God's call of Abram and God's covenant with him (Gen 15). Like Moses, Abraham rationally and verbally communicated with God, which served as the basis for Abraham's life mission. He understood and trusted God. "Abram believed the LORD, and he credited it to him as righteousness" (Gen 15:6).

I chose a sentence from the account of the burning bush in Exodus because this was the first time God revealed his essential name and nature. God later said to Moses, "I am the LORD. I appeared to Abraham, to Isaac and to Jacob as God Almighty, but by my name the LORD I did not make myself fully known to

---

[9]See also James 1:17; Hebrews 1:12; 13:8.

them" (Ex 6:2-3). Upon that name and nature, Yahweh would make further covenants with his people, holding them accountable to his revelation to them. A covenant is more than a contract. God's covenants are unilaterally offered by God himself and obligate those receiving them to obey their stipulations and be blessed or to disobey and be cursed. God will uphold his part of the contract. These covenants bring forth a people, a nation, a group held together more by belief, learning, and tradition than by blood or by soil.

God establishes four explicit covenants in the Hebrew Bible.[10] After the flood, with Noah as his witness, God makes a unilateral covenant to never destroy the earth by water and seals it with the rainbow (Gen 9:12-17). The second covenant is when God calls the patriarch Abraham to leave his native country and go to a new land.

> I will make you into a great nation,
>   and I will bless you;
> I will make your name great,
>   and you will be a blessing. (Gen 12:2)

God's word came to pass, but his people found themselves trapped in the bondage of Egypt under "a new king, to whom Joseph meant nothing" (Ex 1:8). Then God raised up Moses and made a third covenant with him and his people. God made a fourth covenant with David, which would prove pivotal for the coming Messiah, who would be the son of David (2 Sam 7).

The Mosaic Covenant hinges on the giving of the Ten Commandments or Decalogue. How the Hebrews responded to

---

[10]Some Calvinist theologians speak of a "covenant of works" enacted in the garden before the fall, but this is an inference and is not directly stated in the text. See R. C. Sproul, "The Covenant of Works," *Table Talk*, June 8, 2022, www.ligonier.org/learn/articles /covenant-works.

these commands would determine their fate. Decalogue means "the ten words." Thus, the Jewish emphasis on words spoken by God continues. We read this in the prologue: "And God spoke all these words: 'I am the LORD your God, who brought you out of Egypt, out of the land of slavery'" (Ex 20:1-2). The God who spoke of his name, and thus his character, now speaks of his gracious deliverance of his people out of Egypt and how they ought to live given God's character (Ex 20:3-18).

WORDS AND IMAGES

After forbidding other gods, God commands something almost universally ignored in the contemporary world:

> You shall not make for yourself an image in the form of anything in heaven above or on the earth beneath or in the waters below. You shall not bow down to them or worship them. (Ex 20:4-5)

There is dispute whether this forbids merely the worship of images or forbids any images of God at all. It may appear to forbid any images at all, but that does not square with the images that God commands to be in the temple and tabernacle.[11] Moreover, another passage makes clear that the problem is not representational art per se but the worship of images. God says:

> Do not make idols or set up an image or a sacred stone for yourselves, and do not place a carved stone in your land to bow down before it. I am the LORD your God. (Lev 26:1)

This is reinforced when Moses says, "Then the LORD spoke to you out of the fire. You heard the sound of words but saw no form; there was only a voice" (Deut 4:12).

---

[11]Francis A. Schaeffer, *Art and the Bible*, rev. ed., IVP Classics (Downers Grove, IL: InterVarsity Press, 2006), 20-30, Kindle.

Jewish media theorist and social critic Neil Postman (1931–2003) pondered the second commandment's significance for the God of the Jews and his ways and for us today:

> It is a strange injunction to include as part of an ethical system unless its author assumed a connection between forms of human communication and the quality of a culture. We may hazard a guess that a people who are being asked to embrace an abstract, universal deity would be rendered unfit to do so by the habit of drawing pictures or making statues or depicting their ideas in any concrete, iconographic forms. The God of the Jews was to exist in the Word and through the Word, an unprecedented conception requiring the highest order of abstract thinking.[12]

When Postman writes that God "was to exist in the Word and through the Word," he does not limit God's existence to words but emphasizes the necessity and primacy of written and spoken communication for "the God of the Jews." This insistence that God speaks and must be heard and heeded finds its source in Yahweh, the God who names himself and speaks according to that name. The prohibition of idols and the primacy of the word have shaped Western civilization and served as the foundation of Christianity. But Postman warns us: "People like ourselves who are in the process of converting their culture from word-centered to image-centered might profit by reflecting on this Mosaic injunction."[13] This is an understatement, as his book from which this quote is taken, *Amusing Ourselves to Death*, makes indisputable. One gift from the Jews—or from God, really—is their iconoclasm and insistence that words can

---

[12]Neil Postman, *Amusing Ourselves to Death*, new intro. by Andrew Postman (New York: Penguin, 2006), 9, Kindle.

[13]Postman, *Amusing Ourselves to Death*, 9.

accomplish intellectual work that images cannot accomplish.[14] Sadly, this intellectual inheritance has been squandered in the West, given the decline in reading and the ignorance of history and the great ideas of Western civilization.

The Jews of the Bible period, and ever since, have treasured and studied their sacred texts and ardently passed down this learning throughout the generations, as Deuteronomy instructed.

> These are the commands, decrees and laws the LORD your God directed me to teach you to observe in the land that you are crossing the Jordan to possess, so that you, your children and their children after them may fear the LORD your God as long as you live by keeping all his decrees and commands that I give you, and so that you may enjoy long life. Hear, Israel, and be careful to obey so that it may go well with you and that you may increase greatly in a land flowing with milk and honey, just as the LORD, the God of your ancestors, promised you.
>
> Hear, O Israel: The LORD our God, the LORD is one. Love the LORD your God with all your heart and with all your soul and with all your strength. These commandments that I give you today are to be on your hearts. Impress them on your children. Talk about them when you sit at home and when you walk along the road, when you lie down and when you get up. Tie them as symbols on your hands and bind them on your foreheads. Write them on the doorframes of your houses and on your gates. (Deut 6:1-9; see also Eph 6:1-4).

It is beyond remarkable that the Jews still exist as a people and Judaism exists as a religion. (I make this distinction since some

---

[14]See also Jacques Ellul, *The Humiliation of the Word*, trans. Joyce Main Hanks (Eugene, OR: Wipf and Stock, 2021).

identify as Jews ethnically but lack belief in *I am who I am*.) This is due to their cross-generational tenacity and courage in preserving their beliefs and customs through ritual. In the seventeenth century, Blaise Pascal (1623–1662) took the "perpetuity" of the Jews as a sign of God's revelation to them and of his providence over history in preserving them from the time of the Hebrew Bible to his own day.[15] Through centuries of discrimination, pogroms, expulsions, and even the Nazi attempt to completely exterminate them through "the final solution," the Jewish people have suffered long, endured, and thrived, though their numbers are small relative to other world religions. They reclaimed their homeland in 1948, against all odds. They have defended and retained their homeland against all odds as well. They have weathered antisemitism (which is on the rise), but the Jews continue to be Jews, to relish their heritage, and to be a model of assiduous scholarship, deep learning, and vigorous culture to the world.

While Judaism in its various branches harks back to the "word of God," it treasures its teachings through a deep system of symbols, ceremonies, rites of passage, and other rituals. The word is made visible in the celebration of the Passover, for example, which has been celebrated continuously for three thousand years.[16]

The great Jewish philosopher Maimonides (1138–1204) summarized what all Jews should believe. This is significant since Judaism is a religion based on what God has revealed in history to human beings. Things are not left vague, mysterious, enigmatic, or indeterminate. While some Jews dispute his summary,

---

[15]Blaise Pascal, "Perpetuity," "Proofs of Moses," etc., in *Pensées*, trans. A. J. Krailsheimer (New York Penguin, 1966).

[16]For an explanation of these facets of Judaism, see Winfried Corduan, "Judaism," in *Neighboring Faiths*, 2nd ed. (Downers Grove, IL: IVP Academic, 2012).

these "thirteen principles of faith" have been used in the Jewish prayer book since the early sixteenth century.[17] I have summarized them. They all begin with, "I believe in perfect faith that . . ." and add "blessed be his name" after every reference to the Creator.

1. The Creator is the Author and Guide of everything that has been created, and that he alone has made, does make, and will make all things.

2. The Creator is a Unity, and that there is no unity in any manner like unto his, and that he alone is our God, who was, is, and will be.

3. The Creator is not a body, and that he is free from all the accidents of matter, and that he has no form whatsoever.

4. The Creator is the first and the last.

5. To the Creator and to him alone, it is right to pray, and that it is not right to pray to any being beside him.

6. All the words of the prophets are true.

7. The prophecy of Moses our teacher peace be unto him, was true, and that he was the chief of the prophets, both of those that preceded him and of those who followed him.

8. The whole Law, now in our possession, is the same that was given to Moses our teacher, peace be upon him.

9. His Law will not be changed, and that there will never be any other law from the Creator.

10. The Creator knows every deed of the children of men, and all their thoughts, as it is said, It is he that fashioneth the heart of them all, that giveth heed to all their deeds.

11. The Creator rewards those that keep his commandments and punishes those that transgress them.

---

[17]Ian S. Markham, ed., *A World Religions Reader*, 2nd ed. (Malden, MA: Blackwell, 2000), 234.

12. In the coming of the Messiah, and, though he tarry, I will wait daily for his coming.

13. There will be a resurrection of the dead at the time when it shall please the Creator.[18]

These kinds of affirmations about God's nature, the world, human beings, ethics, history, and eschatology could not be stated without the confidence that God had spoken to humanity, from the burning bush and beyond through the prophets and in the Hebrew Scriptures.[19] To anticipate a later chapter, consider that Christians agree completely with propositions 1, 3-6, 8, 10, 11, and 13.[20] Concerning proposition 2, Christians affirm the oneness of God, but in the unity of the Trinity. Regarding proposition 12, Christians believe the Messiah has come, but they "wait daily for his coming" *again* (or second coming). Concerning 7, Christians affirm that Moses was a great prophet, but Jesus affirmed John the Baptist the greatest of all the prophets of the old covenant (Mt 11:11).

THE PROPHETIC WORD

Maimonides esteemed Moses as the greatest prophet (although the story of Moses is found in the Law, not in the Prophets).[21] This is because God spoke to him, and he, in turn, spoke for

---

[18]Markham, *World Religions Reader,* 234-35.

[19]It is odd that Jewish philosopher Martin Buber, according to Walter Kaufmann, issued "a sharp attack on all talk about God and all pretensions to knowledge about God." Martin Buber, *I and Thou,* trans. Walter Kaufmann (New York: Charles Scribner's Sons, 1970), 20-21, Kindle.

[20]In the incarnation, God remained the immaterial God, but took on a human nature, which includes a body. We might say that God became embodied, but without ceasing to be a pure Spirit. This is explained in the hypostatic union of the two natures of Jesus Christ.

[21]Moses' words are also found in Psalm 90, the only psalm attributed to him.

God to the people and down the ages. Abraham Heschel, the great Jewish philosopher, understood prophecy as *"exegesis of existence from a divine perspective."*[22] God revealed not only true propositions to Moses but his "divine pathos." God is a personal being who has feelings about his creatures. Philosophers, Jewish or otherwise, have debated this, but a straightforward reading of the Hebrew Bible anchors the reality of God's perfectly calibrated affective response to individuals, groups, nations, and history.

Heschel's two-volume masterpiece called *The Prophets* explained and defended the "divine pathos" in depth and with compelling clarity. The biblical prophets were not dispassionate oracles of an abstract deity but were, rather, seized by God's passion for a world of injustice that demanded repentance, restitution, and restoration. They prophesied in striking and vivid language and had eyes to see and ears to hear cruelty and dishonesty that most turned a blind eye to. Their standard was the law that God revealed, and they held God's people accountable to the term of his covenants with them. But they did not simply apply a divine standard to a human situation; they denounced evil and demanded justice, speaking from the very heart of God.

While Greek philosophical tradition—whether Platonic or Aristotelian or Stoic—aligned the perfect with the unchanging, unmovable, and imperturbable, the prophets felt the divine passion for justice and truth to an extent unrivaled in other religious literature.[23] Consider Amos, the prophet:

---

[22]Heschel, *Prophets*, 1:xii.

[23]Heschel's reflections on the difference between the God of the Greek philosophers (and some Jews and Christians) with the God of the prophets is telling and compelling overall. See Heschel, "The Theology of Pathos" and "Comparisons and Contrasts" in *The Prophets*.

Hear this, you who trample the needy
    and do away with the poor of the land,
saying,
"When will the New Moon be over
    that we may sell grain,
and the Sabbath be ended
    that we may market wheat?"—
skimping on the measure,
    boosting the price
and cheating with dishonest scales,
buying the poor with silver
    and the needy for a pair of sandals,
    selling even the sweepings with the wheat. (Amos 8:4-6)

The prophets were never lost in mystical contemplation of the divine but felt viscerally God's displeasure with sin, individual and national. Isaiah's incomparable vision of God dressed in divine majesty and worshiped as "holy, holy, holy," and by angels was not an end in itself but the beginning of his prophetic mission (Is 6:1-7). After God forgave Isaiah's sin (he is a "man of unclean lips"), his first words to him are, "Whom shall I send? And who will go for us?" Isaiah replied, "Here am I. Send me!" (Is 6:8). Thereafter, Isaiah receives his marching orders to speak to this "people of unclean lips" (Is 6:5).

The prophets did not intuit sacred mysteries or reason their way to the will of God.[24] Rather, the word of God came to them. God says to Jeremiah:

The word of the LORD came to me, saying,

"Before I formed you in the womb I knew you,
    before you were born I set you apart;
    I appointed you as a prophet to the nations." (Jer 1:4-5)

---

[24]This does not imply that they prophesied anything irrational; rather, the source of their knowledge was not from human wisdom or patterns of inferential reasoning.

Or consider the prophet Amos.

The words of Amos, one of the shepherds of Tekoa—the vision he saw concerning Israel two years before the earthquake, when Uzziah was king of Judah and Jeroboam son of Jehoash was king of Israel. (Amos 1:1)

So, too, with Ezekiel.

On the fifth of the month—it was the fifth year of the exile of King Jehoiachin—the word of the LORD came to Ezekiel the priest, the son of Buzi, by the Kebar River in the land of the Babylonians. There the hand of the LORD was on him. (Ezek 1:2-3)

Ezekiel received an elaborate vision of God, but "the word of the LORD" is what defined his prophetic mission to a people who "are obstinate and stubborn" (Ezek 2:4). One could summon any of the prophets regarding the power of God's word, but we will further consider Ezekiel's prophetic confidence in God's word.

"Say to them, 'This is what the Sovereign LORD says.' And whether they listen or fail to listen—for they are a rebellious people—they will know that a prophet has been among them. And you, son of man, do not be afraid of them or their words. Do not be afraid, though briers and thorns are all around you and you live among scorpions. Do not be afraid of what they say or be terrified by them, though they are a rebellious people. You must speak my words to them, whether they listen or fail to listen, for they are rebellious." (Ezek 2:4-7).

It was the word of the Sovereign LORD that gave Ezekiel courage and resolve, irrespective of the outcome of his warnings and exhortations to this rebellious people. So, too, for all the prophets as they railed against greed, dishonesty, false religion, and moral complacency. They gave comfort based on God's compassion, but not before putting the fear of God into the hearts of the rebellious.

JUDAISM, GOD, AND THE WORD

Many other aspects of Judaism could be explored, particularly its idea of sacrifice and atonement, the nature of its covenants and how the idea of covenant has helped shape the developments of republics in Western culture,[25] and much more. Nevertheless, without God's self-revelation in true and understandable words, there would be no Judaism. Neither would the Western world have valued the power of words to convey reality as it has historically. Yes, the Greeks contributed greatly to the significance of words for philosophical reasoning, but their notions were never harnessed to a sovereign LORD who spoke, acted, and judged with truth, justice, and grace. The Greeks, at their best, knew something of God, but they never heard the voice of God declaring his name and nature in a burning bush or through the impassioned words of a prophet. That is a gift of the Jews and of their God, who speaks his name.

---

[25]See Os Guinness, *The Magna Carta of Humanity* (Downers Grove, IL: InterVarsity Press, 2021).

- three -

HINDUISM

"You are that."

Hinduism is the dominant—although not the official—religion of India.[1] Perhaps more than any other religion, besides Judaism, it is identified with a nation. But, despite its recognizability, Hinduism is a deep and murky well whose bottom is hard to find. And that well is surrounded by a thick and tangled forest of differing doctrines, practices, and histories. While every religion has different expressions, the heart of Hinduism is obscure. If you claim to have found it, someone, Hindu or otherwise, will likely say you missed it. Therefore, finding one sentence as an entry point into Hinduism will be contested. But to avoid undue criticism and acrimony, I will defend and qualify the sentence selection as we progress.

---

[1] As of this writing, Prime Minister Narendra Modi, an ardent Hindu, is trying to move India in the direction of Hindu nationalism, and churches are suffering for it. See Jeffrey Gettleman and Suhasini Raj, "Arrests, Beatings, and Secret Prayers: Inside the Persecution of India's Christians," *New York Times*, December 22, 2021, www.nytimes.com/2021/12/22/world/asia/india-christians-attacked.html.

The sentence has but three words in English: *You are that.* The older translation, with a King James ring, was "Thou art that." The original Sanskrit rendering is *Tat Tvam Asi* and is taken from a dialogue in the Chandogya Upanishad (600 BC) where it is repeated six times.

Unlike Christianity, Islam, and Buddhism, Hinduism does not have a founding figure akin to Jesus, Muhammad, or Buddha.[2] Nor can it invoke several deeply historical and formative figures at its origin or in its development, as can Judaism with Abraham, Moses, David, and the prophets. Hinduism's cast of characters is colorful indeed. Krishna, the protagonist of the *Bhagavad Gita*, is often depicted with blue skin, which is telling. I used the word *protagonist* for Krishna since that word usually denotes the leading character in a work of fiction—a point to which we will return.

Another difficulty is that while Hinduism has sacred writings, its corpus is huge, varied, and not approached in the same sense that the monotheistic religions revere their Scriptures—the Hebrew Bible, the New Testament, and the Qur'an. The later books are taken to be the inspired communication from a personal and rational God. As such, they are amenable to protracted intellectual engagement through exegesis and theologizing. Hinduism has its Scripture scholars, but they are generally not seeking the mind of God in the sense that monotheistic scholars are through their interactions with the text. (Consider the chapters that discuss the concept of revelation in Judaism, Christianity, and Islam.)

---

[2]Two other world religions have identifiable founders, Mahavira for Jainism and Zoroaster for Zoroastrianism, but this short book does not discuss these religions. See Winfried Corduan, *Neighboring Faiths*, 2nd ed. (Downers Grove, IL: IVP Academic, 2012), chaps. 11, 6.

A Big Tent with Six Pegs

Before discussing some of the differences of belief among Hindus and the meaning of *You are that*, the pegs of Hinduism's big tent need to be staked into the ground. In a work on yoga, historian and philosopher of religion Mircea Eliade (1907–1986) states that Hindus share the following six beliefs.[3]

First, the four Vedas are deemed sacred Scripture. These are the oldest of the Hindu texts. Unlike monotheistic religions, which claim that revelation was given in history to individuals or a nation (as with Israel), Hinduism teaches that the Vedas had always existed but were apprehended by sages in mystical states, passed down through oral tradition, and then committed to writing between about 1500 and 500 BC. Other texts commonly taken to be sacred are the Upanishads and the *Bhagavad Gita*.

Second, Hindus believe in the wheel of karma, an impersonal system that assigns mortal outcomes to all living things based on the merits or demerits of their previous lifetimes. This is called transmigration since the souls of beings migrate from one state to another state from lifetime to lifetime. The wheel includes all forms of life, not just human beings.

Third, Hindus believe that karma and reincarnation fix a person's status in each of his or her lifetimes. This caste system is divided into four groups: Brahmins are the highest caste and are commonly priests and teachers. Kshatriyas are known traditionally as warriors. The Vaishyas are the merchant class. The Shudras constitute the lowest caste and are manual labors. Outside of the system entirely are the Dalits or untouchables, many of whom have left Hinduism in the past twenty years for Christianity or Buddhism.

---

[3]Mircea Eliade, *Yoga: Immortality and Freedom*, trans. Willard R. Trask (Princeton, NJ: Princeton University Press, 1958), 3.

Fourth, Hinduism teaches that our common perception and understanding of reality is clouded by maya or illusion. The meaning of *maya* is interpreted variously, but it refers to a fundamental misunderstanding of reality that obscures the sacred and inhibits spiritual liberation.

Yoga is the fifth commonality among Hindus. The term is usually associated with Buddhism, but its origins are Hindu, and its meaning is spiritual liberation from the bonds of mortality and matter such that one is freed from the wheel of karma, never to suffer again. Sometimes, the term *moksha* is used.

Sixth, the way to Nirvana or *moksha* is through yoga or spiritual discipline of some kind. Jnana yoga pursues divine knowledge through meditation. Bhakti yoga is personal devotion to a God (such as Krishna). Karma yoga is the way of good works. In America, yoga is usually known as a physical discipline of stretching and, in some cases, chanting.[4]

While all Hindus hold these six beliefs, they are affirmed within wildly divergent metaphysical systems. Some, perhaps most, Hindus are polytheistic, taking a particular god (such as Krishna) for themselves or their family. They offer gifts and devotion to one god or goddess. Some are monotheistic, believing in one personal god. This is the bhakti tradition, which involves worship. (Monotheism is a variant of Hinduism; it is not at its essence.) There is even an atheistic school of Hinduism (*samkhya*). Other Hindus are nondualistic or monistic, believing that there is but one, impersonal reality called Brahman.

---

[4]I have argued elsewhere that yoga, given its Hindu origin and nature, is not an appropriate discipline for Christians. See Douglas Groothuis, "Spiritual Dangers of New Age Meditation and Yoga," blog, March 22, 2021, https://douglasgroothuis.com/post/spiritual-dangers-of-new-age-meditation-and-yoga.

Of course, like all religions, Hinduism is not merely a set of beliefs. In fact, it is far less creed oriented than monotheistic religions. A thorough introduction would explain its rites of passage, sacred celebrations, temple observations, and other means of worship.[5] But our focus will be on a statement—*You are that*—that sums up nondualistic Hinduism.

This sentence is used to support one school of Hinduism, called Advaita Vedanta, which advances the metaphysic of monism or nondualism in addition to pantheism. *Monism*, as the name suggests, means that all is one (*mono*). *Monotheism* means there is one infinite personal God. *Monism* means there is one divine reality that admits of no duality between one person and another, between humanity and nature, or between nature and the divine. Put differently and negatively, reality is nondual. Think of taking a mystical eraser to all the boundaries that separate things. What is left is the Supreme Self or Brahman. But let us get to our sentence, its explication, and its implications.

WHAT IS "THAT"?

Our sentence comes in a dialogue between a father and a son contained in one of the twelve Upanishads. After the son asks his father to instruct him in wisdom, the father replies.

In the beginning was only Being,
One without a second.
Out of himself he brought forth the cosmos
And entered into everything in it.
There is nothing that does not come from him.
Of everything he is the inmost Self.

---

[5]See Corduan, "Hinduism," in *Neighboring Faiths.*

He is the truth; he is the Self supreme.
You are that, Shvetaketu; you are that.[6]

This and related texts have been read several ways, but there are several nonnegotiable aspects. First, the original Being is "One without a second." The idea of oneness or nondualism is crucial to this passage and to Advaita Vedanta Hinduism. Second, the cosmos emanates from this Being, and he is everything's inmost Self or essence. Third, Shvetaketus is *identified* with the Self supreme. The father is not saying that his son is part of this Being or that part of the son is one with this Being. Rather, the Self supreme is one with the son and with everything else. The text refers to Being and Self supreme as "himself," but "itself" is probably a better description.

These statements, and others like them, have traditionally been interpreted by saying that "Atman is Brahman," although those words do not appear in the quotation above. This indicates that the self or individual (the Atman) is really one with the universal or Supreme Self (Brahman).[7] Images such as the wave being one with the ocean gets this across. If we take the wave to be separate from the ocean, we misidentify it and are lost in the world of maya or illusion.

In his foreword to his translation to *The Upanishads*, Eknath Easwarn writes:

This tremendous equation—"the Self is Brahman"—is the central discovery of the Upanishads. Its most famous formulation is one of the *mahavakyas* or "great formulae": *Tat tvam asi*, "You are That." "That" is the characteristic way

---

[6]Eknath Easwaran, trans., *The Upanishads*, 2nd ed. (Tomales, CA: Nilgiri Press, 2007), 133, Kindle.

[7]Atman can also mean the universal Self, but "Atman is Braham" is a common way of saying that self is the Self.

the Upanishads point to a Reality that cannot be described; and "you," of course, is not the petty, finite personality, but that pure consciousness "which makes the eye see and the mind think": the Self.[8]

A philosophical distinction about the word *is* helps explain this stupendous claim of the Upanishads. If I say, "Sunny is brown haired," I am using the *is* of predication. That is, I am attributing or predicating of my dog, Sunny, the feature or quality of having brown hair. Classically, this is put as S (the subject) is P (the predicate). Of course, I could ascribe other predicates to my beloved pup: cute, funny, happy, emotionally sensitive, and so on.

Now consider another *is* statement: "Sunny is Sunny." This mundane statement illustrates the law of identity. Something is and only is what it is, and not something else. Or: A is A. The *is* used in "Sunny is Sunny" is, not surprisingly, the *is* of identity. It gets more interesting if we use another illustration: "Douglas Groothuis is the son of Harold and Lillian Groothuis." Douglas Groothuis and "the son of Harold and Lillian Groothuis" mean the same thing and refer to the same entity. This is not like saying, "Douglas Groothuis has brown hair," which is the *is* of predication. Predication is not symmetrical; that is, brown hair is not the same as Douglas Groothuis, but Douglas Groothuis is the same as the son of Harold and Lillian Groothuis.

J. P. Moreland further expands on this in explaining the two senses of *is*.

Identity is a relation which is *reflexive* (A is identical to itself), *symmetrical* (if A is identical to B, then B is identical to A), and *transitive* (if A is identical to B, and B is identical

---

[8]Easwaran, *Upanishads*, 38-39.

to C, then A is identical to C). If A and B are identical, then whatever is true of A is true of B and vice versa.[9]

We walked down this analytical avenue only to find *You are that* at the end of it. According to nondualistic Hinduism, *You are that* uses the *is* of identity. Although the word *is* won't be found in *You are that* (given the grammar), the sentence specifies this meaning; thus, it can be reworded as: "The self is that"— with "that" meaning Self or Brahman. For simplicity and readability, we will use Self. Or we might advert to the synonymous saying, "Atman is Brahman."

Let us plug in Moreland's threefold breakdown of the *is* of identity.

1. The self (Atman) is identical to itself (reflexivity).
2. The Self (Brahman) is identical to itself (reflexivity).
3. Whatever is true of the self, is true of the Self (symmetry).
4. The self is the Self; thus, every other self is the Self as well (transitivity).

Since (1) and (2) are truisms, we will consider (3) and (4).

5. If (3), then each self cannot be a "petty, finite" self but is actually one with the Self, which is "a Reality that cannot be described" and is "pure consciousness"—in other words, Self.
6. If (5), then the self does not exist qua the self. Any limiting quality of the self (petty, finite, mortal, lacking pure consciousness) is an illusion.
7. But the self is not an illusion since we experience ourselves as petty, finite, etc.—all qualities that the Self lacks.
8. Concerning (4), other selves experience themselves as petty, finite, mortal, and lacking pure consciousness.

---

[9]J. P. Moreland, *Scaling the Secular City: A Defense of Christianity* (Grand Rapids, MI: Baker Books, 1987), 39-40, emphasis added.

9. Each individual self also experiences other selves as petty, finite, etc.

10. Therefore (a) there is no symmetry between the self and the Self.

11. Therefore (b) there is no transitivity between any self and any other self as the Self.

12. Therefore (c) *You are that* (the self is the Self or Atman is Brahman) is false.

13. Therefore (d) nondualistic Hinduism is false.

Another philosophical principle calls out to us: the *identity of indiscernibles*, first stated by the philosopher Gottfried Wilhelm Leibniz. Two things indiscernible in their qualities are really the same thing under different names. If X has only qualities p, q, and r and Y has only qualities p, q, and r, then X and Y are the same entity but with two different names. The identity of indiscernible is, for Leibniz, an a priori principle.

Now consider *You are that* or "The self is the Self." If the self and the Self share all the same qualities, then they are identical. Nothing differentiates them. However, to speak of self in relation to Self is to introduce differentiating qualities, as mentioned above. The self is "petty, finite," and so on. But the Self is not these things. Thus, explaining the *is* of identity in relation to the identity of indiscernibles shows that nondualism is in double trouble metaphysically.

It seems the only hope of rescuing *You are that* logically is to claim that (7) is false; that is, the self is an illusion, the product of maya. This is a hard claim to establish since we constantly experience ourselves as limited beings interacting with other limited beings. These experiences are incorrigible. To deny (7) means that metaphysical individuation (there are many limited and individual beings in the world) is simply false.

I once heard a nondualist philosopher claim to have attained nondualistic consciousness for some time but lost it because of a physical injury. Yet, if the world of individual things is unreal and the Self alone is real, there would be nothing in existence to bring him out of nondual consciousness (or perfect consciousness). Pain, morality, pettiness, and the rest are mere maya and should have no hold over us as objective realities. Thus, his account is illogical and, thus, false.

INEFFABILITY

Indulge another stroll down Analytic Avenue to critique the claim made above that the Self "is a Reality that cannot be described." This concerns *ineffability*—the attempt to speak and reason about what cannot be spoken of or reasoned about. Here is how it plays out.

1. The Self is a Reality that cannot be described.
2. If (1), therefore (a) there is no reason to capitalize Reality or Self since it cannot be described. Capitalized Reality or Self could not be distinguished from noncapitalized reality or self since the former cannot be described. What cannot be described cannot be said to be better than something that is described, such as "the petty self."
3. If (1), therefore (b) the self cannot be identical to the Self since what cannot be described cannot be said to be identical to (or different from) anything.
4. Therefore (c) the claim that "the Self is a reality that cannot be described" is false.
5. Given (4), therefore (d) the self cannot be identical to the Self. This is because a relationship of identity cannot be established between a known (finite, petty self) and the unknown and unknowable Brahman (Self).

We now move from philosophical analysis to a personal testimony. Although nondualism falls on hard times logically, it is often offered to the uninitiated as an experience beyond logic rather than as the result of reasoned argument and evidence.

My Guru Encounter

I experienced the nondualistic Hindu mindset at work when I attended a lecture by Chinmoy Kumar Ghose (a.k.a., Sri Chinmoy, 1931–2007), who was the guru of guitarists John McLaughlin and Carlos Santana. I was transfixed by the genre-shattering and virtuoso music of McLaughlin's group, The Mahavishnu Orchestra (1971–1973), a few years earlier, and I knew that Chinmoy was an inspiration for McLaughlin to quit drugs and practice meditation. My hearing of the group's first album, "The Inner Mounting Flame" (1971), was something of a spiritual experience (as it was for many). *Mahavishnu* was the Sanskrit name that Chinmoy gave McLaughlin. It means "the great Vishnu" (a Hindu god). McLaughlin's playing took a quantum leap in creativity and intensity after his submission to his guru, and his musical compositions were mind-boggling and compelling. Santana's music progressed as well. One haunting piece by the Mahavishnu Orchestra was called "The Dance of Maya," with clear reference to the Hindu doctrine of illusion. So I wondered if this indicated a spiritual reality worth pursuing.

When I saw Chinmoy, he appeared in flowing white guru garb and was accompanied by several young and worshipful devotees dressed in Indian clothing. I cannot remember much of what Chinmoy said since he didn't say much of anything. He was speaking into the air more than to us. This was part of the guru-chic of the day. I do remember him saying, "Doubt is poison," but no context was given. After a number of vapid aphorisms, a man in the audience asked him, "Sir, what is your teaching? What do you want us to know?" The guru said without emotion, "I have written many books. I have traveled the world." He then began chanting "Ohm"—the meditative mantra used to indicate and access the oneness of reality and to denote the vacuity of the rational mind to perceive it. His eyes rolled back into his head as he continued to chant for several minutes. I was not a Christian at the time, but it spooked me. My girlfriend, who came with me, said she couldn't stop looking into his eyes. I said I could not look into his eyes. We broke up shortly after that.

This high school memory illustrates that nondualism claims that the ultimate reality of Self is not accessible through normal patterns of reasoning or communication. Chanting is the answer. Words fail of necessity. Yet, if someone asks me, "Sir, what is your teaching? What do you want us to know?," I could explain the gospel in one minute (as I once did for a podcast) or in one hour, or I could give him or her a Bible. There is so much to say and only one short life in which to say it. As Jesus said, "What I tell you in the dark, speak in the daylight; what is whispered in your ear, proclaim from the roofs" (Mt 10:27). But we must return to philosophical examination.

ONE REALITY, BUT TWO TRUTHS?[10]

The great nondualist philosopher Sankara (788–830) attempted to advance a two-truth theory to accommodate the seeming reality of the self in relation to the ultimate reality of the Self. He argued that there is a relative reality in which saying things like "I exist as a petty self and others exist as petty selves" can be true in its place. However, in the ultimate reality of Self, these statements are not true. Thus, Sankara wants to give some standing

---

[10]What follows is adapted from Douglas Groothuis, "Sankara's Two-Level View of Truth: Nondualism on Trial," *Journal of the International Society of Christian Apologetics* 1, no. 1 (2008): 105-12.

to the phenomenal world of non-Self, but only in a relation with the ultimate reality of the Self. In this way, he can affirm *You are that* coherently since the *you* occupies a lower and nonultimate place metaphysically. In so doing, Sankara tries to avoid the contradictions I articulated above. Sankara wanted to circumvent the charge that the lower level was an absolute illusion of nonbeing.

Sankara argued that the world of maya is a world of subjects apprehending external objects.

> The non-existence of external things cannot be maintained because we are conscious of external things. In every act of perception we are conscious of some external thing corresponding to the idea, whether it be a post or a wall or a piece of cloth or a jar, and that of which we are conscious cannot but exist.[11]

I agree. Yet if Brahman alone is truly real as the sole Being, where does the world of eternal things and tawdry selves fit? Sankara tries to reconcile his understanding of the objective world of individuated things perceived by individual beings with the final reality of nondualism by virtue of a two-level theory of truth. For the unenlightened, the plural world seems to be the ultimate reality. But those who practice *jñana marga* (the way of knowledge) and attain a "cognition of the infinite" transcend this lower level to attain to spiritual release (*moksha*) by gaining knowledge (*vidya*). We will consider the two-truth view in two dimensions.[12]

---

[11]Sankara, *Commentary on Brhad-aranyaka Upanishad*, IV,4,6, quoted in Eliot Deutsch, *Advaita Vedanta: A Philosophical Reconstruction* (Honolulu: University Press of Hawaii, 1969), 95.

[12]I derive these categories from Stuart C. Hackett's fine study, *Oriental Philosophy: A Westerner's Guide to Eastern Thought* (Madison: University of Wisconsin Press, 1979), chap. 4.

1. Metaphysics is divided into (a) empirical reality: phenomenally real objects and (b) Absolute reality, which is nondual and nondifferentiated.

2. Theology is divided between (a) Saguna Brahman and (b) Nirguna Braham. The word *guna* is quality or attribute in Sanskrit. Saguna Brahman means "Brahman with qualities." Those not fully enlightened will understand Brahman in this way and may worship him with hymns, some of which Sankara himself wrote. Many need to worship and sing hymns because they have not yet transcended this level. Nirguna Brahman means "Brahman without qualities," which is the nondual reality of Self.

The (a) level has only a provisional or relative reality while the (b) level is ultimate. Therefore, Deutsch, a nondualist, comments:

> The whole of perception and reason [the (a) levels above] is negated the moment there is a dawning of the truth of [Nirguna] Brahman [the (b) levels]. *If Brahman alone is real,* then clearly there cannot be another order of truth that subsists in some kind of finality. From the standpoint of Brahman, all other knowledge is *false.*[13]

Notice the qualifying phrase "from the standpoint of Brahman." Sankara wants to argue that from the standpoint of the (a) level there are empirical realities involving different objects, including the self. However, they are not "ultimately real" or "finally true." The great question then becomes, "What is the difference between the 'ultimately real' and the lesser versions of 'reality'?"

Madhva (1197–1276) was a Hindu philosopher who founded a school called Dvaita (or Dualism) that opposed nondualism by

---

[13]Deutsch, *Advaita Vedanta*, 90, emphasis mine.

affirming the ontological difference between Brahman and the self. As well as claiming Sankara had misinterpreted sacred texts, Madhva argued that Sankara's levels-of-truth doctrine was incoherent. There is either a world of plural selves and empirical objects or there is not. It is an either-or. You cannot have it both ways. Madhva appealed to the oneness of truth and assumed the law of bivalence. A declarative statement (one that expresses a proposition) is either true or false. To claim that the statement "There are many selves" is true for one level but not true for another "ultimate" level is illogical for Madhva. I agree. His critique is cogent because ontological claims either correctly describe states of affairs or they fail to do so. It is difficult to rank levels of truth when the higher level contradicts the lower level. Consider the following statements:

1. Actor Will Smith slapped comedian Chris Rock at the 2022 Academy Awards.
2. Will Smith did not slap Chris Rock at the 2022 Academy Awards.
3. Will Smith tried to slap Chris Rock at the 2022 Academy Awards, but Rock ducked and avoided the slap.

Only statement (1) is true because it states a fact. Both statements (2) and (3) are false because they are not factual. Neither of the two false statements are true from any perspective. They are both false. If someone believes either (2) or (3) to be true, he or she is in error. There is no question of "levels of truth" here in the sense Sankara wants to defend. One might say that (3) is closer to the truth than (2) since it includes the slap attempt. Nevertheless, when one knows that (1) is true, then (2) and (3) are negated as false. They are not true in a lower level of reality, nor can either statement (2) or (3) be true on any supposedly higher level of reality either.

Consider another set of statements concerning differing perspectives on states of affairs:

1. On earth, things appear separate from one another, whether people or cities or nations.
2. From outer space the earth appears as one orb; most separations are not visible.

Can these statements be arranged in a way analogous to Sankara's two levels of truth? Statement (1) is not negated by (2). Rather, (1) and (2) are complementary descriptions of the same state of affairs. We are residents on one planet; but we are individuals who are, nevertheless, separable from each other in numerous ways. This is sometimes called soft perspectivism.

Sankara's attempt to rescue logic through a two-level view of truth hits troubled waters because the ultimate reality of Brahman ends up negating and contradicting the appearance of duality (however real it may seem). Consider his statement about Brahman:

> The same highest Brahman constitutes . . . the real nature, i.e. that aspect of it which depends on *fictitious* limiting conditions, is not its real nature. For as long as the individual self does not free itself from [ignorance] in the form of duality—which [ignorance] may be compared to the mistake of him who in twilight mistakes a post for a man— and does not rise to the knowledge of the Self, whose nature is unchangeable, eternal Cognition—which expresses itself in the form "I am Brahman"—so long, it remains the individual soul.[14]

---

[14]From *The Vedanta Sutras of Badarayana with the Commentary of Sankara*, trans. George Thibaut, 2 parts (New York: Dover, 1962), 1.3.19; quoted in David K. Clark and Norman L. Geisler, *Apologetics in the New Age: A Christian Critique of Pantheism* (Grand Rapids, MI: Baker Books, 1989), 165, emphasis mine.

If there is one supreme and nondual reality of Brahman, then any determinative attributes pertaining to duality, individuality, and finitude (whether respecting selves, the physical world, or Saguna Brahman) cannot exist. An object cannot both be finite and infinite in the same respect at the same time (given the law of noncontradiction). Yet this is exactly what the two-truth theory gives us.

1. The individual self is limited and part of a plurality of selves.

2. The Brahman Self is unlimited and absolutely unitary.

How can the word *self* be used in the same or a similar way so as to convey any intelligible meaning in both instances? It is only used in an equivocal sense such that the referents self and Self cannot be the same entity because they possess mutually contradictory properties: infinite/finite, one/many, eternal/temporal, and more. To refer to the individual self as real on only a lower level solves nothing logically. Instead, it simply veils a deeper confusion.

The logical enigmas engendered by nondualism become painfully evident with respect to the doctrines of ignorance (*avidya*) and illusion (maya). What is the explanation for the ever-so-real-appearing world of the senses? There is none because the realm of Brahman consciousness is incommensurate with maya; that is, there is no logical relationship between the two. Deutsch explains that the questions of the "ontological source" of ignorance and illusion cannot be "intelligibly asked," according to Sankara, because "knowledge and ignorance cannot co-exist in the same individual, for they are contradictory, like light and darkness." Deutsch comments on this statement by Sankara:

> Knowledge destroys ignorance, hence, from the standpoint of knowledge, there is no ignorance whose origin stands in question. And when in ignorance, one . . . [cannot]

describe the process by which this ignorance ontologically comes to be.[15]

There are only three possible logical sources for maya. And it seems entirely appropriate to search for an ontological source since the two-level view of truth attempts to grant some sense of reality to the lower level of maya.

1. Maya originates from Brahman.
2. Maya originates from individual selves.
3. Maya originates from nothing.

Concerning (1), Sankara claims that maya mysteriously results from the play (*lila*) of Brahman. Brahman, in a sense, engages in *magic* to produce *maya* (the two words are related in Sanskrit). But this option fails since Brahman cannot be the ontological source of that which contradicts its essence. If there is no duality or principle of difference in "the One without second" (as the Upanishads put it), Brahman cannot be the source of maya. Given nondualism, there is no ontological space for such a reality.

Option (2) explains nothing since individual selves are part of what is to be explained in the first place. Illusion cannot explain illusion. Option (3) is logically impossible to sustain since *ex nihilo nihil fit* (from nothing, nothing comes) eliminates this alternative. Nothing, by definition, has no generative or productive powers.[16] Thus, the conjunction of Self and maya (as nondualism must affirm) is logically impossible and, thereby, false.

---

[15]Quoted in Deutsch, *Advaita Vedanta*, 85.

[16]This differs from the biblical doctrine of creation *ex nihilo*, since all things came from God, although God created matter out of nothing. So, there is an efficient cause, a formal cause, and a final cause, but no material cause. There is scientific and philosophical evidence for creation *ex nihilo*. See Douglas Groothuis, *Christian Apologetics: A Comprehensive Case for Biblical Faith*, 2nd ed. (Downers Grove, IL: InterVarsity Press, 2022), 206-23.

JESUS AND THE AVATARS

Having tried to explain *You are that* in the nondualistic terms of Advaita Vedanta, it is appropriate to consider Hinduism's understanding of the avatar in relation to the Christian idea of the incarnation. Hinduism has nothing official to say about Jesus in its sacred documents. The only major world religion that does is Islam since Jesus is mentioned repeatedly in the Qur'an. However, Hindu thinkers outside of the sacred Scriptures have sometimes tried to include Jesus in the category of an avatar. Vishnu is the divine preserver—along with Brahma, the Creator, and Shiva, the Destroyer—and his divine manifestations are known as avatars. An avatar is a manifestation of a particular god who descends to earth as a human or an animal to restore order and divine knowledge. The most well-known avatar is Krishna, the hero prince of the *Bhagavad Gita*.

While Hinduism as a whole includes the idea of the avatar, its different schools interpret the avatars differently. The bhakti school of Hinduism pursues a personal relationship with a god, such as Krishna. A nondualist would see an avatar as a personal manifestation of the impersonal Brahman, as a path to transcend the self to realize the Self. On this view, Jesus would be a manifestation of Self who teaches others to find the Self within the self, that is, to find the God within. And he is but one among many avatars.

Throughout my forty-five years of teaching and writing about world religions and new religious movements, I have come across myriad attempts to recast Jesus as a pantheistic mystic as opposed to the uniquely divine Savior and Lord who shines through the Bible. My book *Jesus in an Age of Controversy* is dedicated to refuting the pantheistic claim.[17] The short response

---

[17]Douglas Groothuis, *Jesus in an Age of Controversy* (Eugene, OR: Harvest House, 1996). See also Ron Rhodes, *The Counterfeit Christ of the New Age Movement* (Grand Rapids, MI: Baker Books, 1991).

is that in order to excavate a nondualistic Jesus from the New Testament, one must use a distorted method in which the clear meaning of terms is twisted and replaced with statements based on another worldview (2 Pet 3:16). Jesus presents himself and is presented as one-of-a-kind and a once-for-all incarnation (Mt 11:27-30; Jn 3:16; 14:6; Acts 4:12; Eph 1:18-23; 1 Tim 2:5).

As I argue in an upcoming chapter, Jesus was a monotheist who claimed to be one with the *I am who I am* who revealed himself to Moses (Ex 3:14; Jn 8:58). This claim and others are situated in space-time history and not culled from legendary material, as does Hinduism's account of its avatars. Krishna devotee and scholar Mataji Devi Vanamale admits that "Hinduism is not a historical religion. If somebody could prove conclusively that Krishna, Rama, and the various gods of the Hindu pantheon never existed, most Hindus would not mind in the least."[18] For Christians, if Christ never lived, or lived but was not raised from the dead, their religion is refuted as are their hopes for their own resurrection from the dead (1 Cor 15:14-19).

YOU ARE WHAT?

It may seem tendentious to see Hinduism through the prism of one sentence when that sentence has been interpreted several ways and when Hinduism is a big temple with so much Scripture. However, the nondualistic take on *You are that* is ancient and has perennial appeal, even today in America. Many think that by digging deeply enough into them-selves they can find the Self. I once heard the electric jazz bass player Victor Wooten unexpectedly rap out the lyric "I am God" in Boulder Theater

---

[18][Mataji Devi] Vanamali, *The Complete Life of Krishna: Based on Earliest Oral Traditions and the Sacred Scriptures* (Rochester, VT: Inner Traditions, 2012), xiii; quoted in Kenneth Richard Samples, *God Among Sages: Why Jesus Is Not Just Another Religious Leader* (Grand Rapids, MI: Baker Books, 2017), 80.

about ten years ago. I rapped back, "No you're not." Perhaps that was not the best apologetic strategy, but at least I was not asked to leave the premises.

This chapter gives the better apologetic strategy, which I hope has been convincing. You and I are finite selves, and any aspiration beyond that is not enlightenment but self-deception. Any redemption for the "finite and tawdry self" is to be found outside ourselves and not from within ourselves. As Pascal wrote of salvation:

> Be comforted; it is not from within yourself that you must expect it [salvation], but on the contrary you must expect it by expecting nothing from yourself.[19]

---

[19]Pascal, *Pensées*, trans. A. J. Krailsheimer (New York Penguin, 1966), 202 (item 517), 66.

- four -

BUDDHISM

"Life is suffering."

H ow could a religion whose first essential or "noble truth" is *Life is suffering* have endured for twenty-five hundred years and command the faith of approximately 376 million adherents worldwide? Yes, we suffer in this life (as do other living things), but is life itself suffering? Is life so suffused and infused with suffering that we can identify life itself with suffering? Buddhism says yes. In so doing, it says no to any hopes of the world of nature and humans as redeemable. However, Buddhism does offer a way out, as we will see; but that path gives no hope to the world as such, since it must be left behind.

Buddhists may not lead with the line *Life is suffering* when seeking converts, but the truth-claim remains—ineradicable and insistent, nonetheless. While it may not seem so to Americans, Buddhism is one of the three great missionary religions, joined by Christianity and Islam. Buddha urged his followers to take the dharma to the world for its betterment.

Fare ye forth, brethren, on the mission that is for the good of the many, for the happiness of the many; to take compassion to the world; to work for the profit and good and happiness of gods and men. Go singly; go not in pairs.[1]

Buddhism moved from India into what is now Sri Lanka and Southeast Asia, then throughout northern and eastern Asia, and finally into China, Japan, and the United States.[2] It is a global religion intent on converts, although most Americans have not been evangelized. Nevertheless, they have evangelized themselves, given the interest in various aspects of Buddhism today. Behind the recent interest in mindfulness and quieting the mind,[3] which is all the rage in recent years, lies Buddhism's world-denying philosophy: *Life is suffering*. But we are getting ahead of ourselves.

The Man Who Became the Buddha

The worldview of Buddhism is based the teachings of the Buddha. Buddha is a title, which means "the one who woke up." According to Buddhism, a mere man, Siddhartha Gautama (approximately 560—480 BCE), became the Buddha when he was enlightened. What matters most to Buddhism is not so much the Buddha himself but the teaching (or dharma) he propounded. The story goes that a man born into wealth and privilege in northern India in the fifth century BC became disenchanted with his status and

---

[1]Quoted in Harold A. Netland, *Christianity and Religious Diversity* (Grand Rapids, MI: Baker Academic, 2015), 74, Kindle. For another translation with attribution in Buddhist Scripture, see "The Teacher of Gods and Men," *Buddhist Studies: The Buddha & His Disciples*, Buddha Dharma Education Association & BuddhaNet, accessed January 4, 2023, www.buddhanet.net/e-learning/buddhism/disciples06.htm.

[2]Netland, *Christianity and Religious Diversity*, 73-75.

[3]See Sarah C. Geis, "Thinking Through Mindfulness: Psychology, Religion or Both?," *Christian Research Journal*, July 13, 2020, www.equip.org/article/thinking-through-mindfulness-psychology-religion-or-both.

family and sought spiritual enlightenment. His quest was triggered by "the four sights." He beheld a sick man, an old man, a corpse, and an ascetic holy man. Realizing that his comfortable but unfulfilling life must come to an end, he left his young wife and child to pursue salvation alone. Such a decision to abandon family seems scandalous to many, but it is accepted in the Buddhist tradition. While Jesus said that love of God must come before love of family (Mt 10:34-39), he himself did not forfeit any family relationships in his ministry (although he never married) or call his followers to leave their spouses or children. Nor can that be said of Muhammad, however different his familial relationships were, given his polygamy.

But Siddhartha could not find it within his ancestral teachings of Hinduism. After nearly starving himself through asceticism, Siddhartha finally found enlightenment while meditating under a tree. The way he would teach was neither extreme Hindu asceticism nor worldly involvement (even in the highest caste) but rather a "middle way." He thus became "the Buddha," which is a title for one who has awakened. He then commenced to teach his discovery to a small group of male disciples.

Buddha thus fits the category of a religious sage, not an avatar or an incarnation. He did not present himself as any kind of savior but rather offered himself as an example of enlightenment and a teacher of such. (Buddha was later deemed a kind of savior in folk Buddhism, but this fits poorly with the earliest records.) His essential teaching is called "The Four Noble Truths" and is affirmed by every branch of Buddhism.

THE FOUR NOBLE TRUTHS

The First Noble Truth is *Life is suffering* (or *dukkha* in Sanskrit). This claim is not unique to Buddha but is fundamental, in one form or another, to most all Indian philosophy. Americans may struggle to understand this view, given their optimism, boost-erism, and can-do attitude. We want to put suffering into the background or to ignore it completely. Suffering indicates failure. Or we think that failure can be a step toward eventual success. Hence, the endless boosterism and positive thinking of the American tradition. Not so for Buddhism, however. *Life is suffering*, and you should admit it if you want to find enlightenment.

The Buddhist writer Bart Gruzalski calls attention to the meaning of this statement according to a Buddhist worldview, so he is worth quoting at length:

> The Buddha's statement of the First Noble Truth does not take a personal perspective. The Buddha did not say, "we suffer" or "each of us suffers" and then point to birth, illness, separation, death, and all the rest. Instead, he said "there is suffering." He did not say it was mine or yours or that it belonged to anyone. He did not blame suffering on anyone. The First Noble Truth makes a straightforward observation: there is suffering. In the same natural way that rain occurs, winds blow, and the sun rises and sets daily, so too suffering occurs as part of the web of life.[4]

The contrast with the teaching of Jesus and the Bible is enormous at this point, as we will see. Since *Life is suffering* is our chapter's sentence of choice, we will return to it at length.

But the Buddha could not leave it at that. What about suffering? What causes it? The second noble truth is that suffering is caused by desire or craving.[5] We often want what we cannot

---

[4]Bart Gruzalski, *On the Buddha* (Belmont, CA: Wadsworth, 1999), 11.
[5]Some argue that Buddha did not disavow all desire but disavowed only excessive desire (craving). However, the ultimate state of Nirvana seems to be one with no desires whatsoever.

attain and end up experiencing what we do not want. Those are the two faces of suffering, both rooted in desire. We desire health, but we experience illness. We desire a fulfilling relationship, but we are betrayed or ignored. And so it goes in each life and throughout history.

The third noble truth is that suffering can only be addressed by ceasing from desire or craving. One must go to the root. The satisfaction of desires or the elimination of frustrations is never enough to satisfy anyone or to bring final liberation from the world of suffering. Neither the self nor the world can be re-formed or redeemed; thus, they must be rejected by cutting off their source of immiserating power.

Given the depth of attachment between us and the world of impossible satisfactions, a total break will not be easy to find "detachment." The severance requires studied discipline. This may be achieved through "the noble eightfold path," which comprises (1) *the right view* or philosophy of life; (2) *the right intention* or desire to find enlightenment; (3) *right speech* or speaking judiciously; (4) *the right action* or acting judiciously; (5) *the right livelihood*, which for Buddha meant being a monk; (6) *the right effort* or expending energy properly; (7) *the right mindfulness* or proper meditation; and (8) *the right concentration* or keeping a continuous focus on truth.

These eight endeavors are grouped into three categories: namely, (1) moral conduct (right speech, action, and livelihood); (2) mental discipline (right effort, mindfulness, and concentration); and (3) wisdom (right thought and understanding). The goal of this effort is release from the world of suffering entirely. The wheel of suffering (or samsara) through karma and rebirth is broken, and one is free to experience Nirvana forever. Nirvana means what is left when a candle or flame is blown out. It is not a place or a thing but a state of being that Buddhists are loathe to say much about since it is the negation of all that is human and commonplace.

Buddhism and Hinduism Contrasted

Hinduism is a big tent, encompassing many varied beliefs as we have seen. However, it is not infinitely elastic or accommodating. Even Hindus have doctrinal boundaries. While we cannot understand the teaching of the Buddha without the background of Hinduism, we cannot place Buddha within Hinduism for at least three reasons.

First, he denied the sacred status of the Vedas; second, he rejected the caste system. These two doctrines are fundamental and nonnegotiable for Hinduism. Third, Buddha rejected Hinduism in that he found it unable to provide the spiritual liberation that he desired. This centered in Hinduism's affirmation of Brahman as the supreme reality. Although understood differently by various schools of Hinduism, Brahman is often known as the universal Self, as discussed earlier. It is the one and all-encompassing reality, which overwhelms individual identity. Buddha took the polar opposite position. There is no self in any substantial sense. What we take as an enduring self—that we can satisfy through fulfilling desires—is an illusion, a collection of separate aggregates called *skandhas*. Buddhists liken the parts of the supposed self to the parts of a chariot. They all compose the chariot, but none of them is the essence of it. The chariot, like the self, is a collection, not a substance. The reality is the no-self (*anatta*) since nothing endures over time. This is the doctrine of impermanence (*anicca*).

The teachings of the Buddha were originally meant for male monks, who would utterly devote themselves to finding enlightenment. They would not work but would beg for food. Eventually, the ethics of Buddhism divided into a code for laypeople and one for monks that included more instruction.

Monks vow to follow the Ten Precepts:

1. not to take any life (the principle of *ahimsa*)
2. not to steal
3. not to commit sexual immorality
4. not to lie
5. not to take intoxicants
6. not to eat in excess or after noon
7. not to attend any entertainments, such as dancing, singing, or drama
8. not to decorate oneself or use cosmetics
9. not to sleep in high or wide beds
10. not to touch any gold or silver[6]

As Buddhism developed, provision was made for nonmonks to be Buddhists. They were exempt from always obeying the ascetic precepts six through ten. But the monks had the inside track on attaining Nirvana, given the rigors of their discipline. Rather than explaining the development of Mahayana Buddhism from the original Theravada school and explaining the other off-shoots, such as Zen, let us consider what is central in Buddhism—the badness and hopelessness of existence and the need to escape it through one's own efforts.

The Buddha's purported last words at age eighty were to "strive diligently for salvation." Buddha offered the dharma of liberation and provided a model, but he offered no vicarious help and no word from God since the existence of God was of no account to him.[7] It was not an edifying question. More

---

[6]Winfried Corduan, *Neighboring Faiths*, 2nd ed. (Downers Grove, IL: IVP Academic, 2012), 322-23, Kindle.

[7]Later Mahayana Buddhism developed the idea of the bodhisattva, one who denies Nirvana to help others find it, but this may not be part of the original teaching. There is even a branch called Pure Land Buddhism, which refers to a heavenly Buddha who

pressing is the removal of suffering from the human condition. If a flaming arrow lodges in your body, you do not ask where it came from but try to remove it. Buddhism is a response to suffering, not an attempt to explain its origins. Nor is the Buddhist idea of rebirth ultimately offered as a way to balance the cosmic scales of good and evil through karmic reward or punishment. Rather, it is a cycle from which one should escape entirely by attaining Nirvana. At best, it is a necessary ladder off this world and into the void since that is better than suffering, life after life.

For Buddhism, even a life of health, wealth, wisdom, talent, and meaning is still a life of suffering since it ends in death and one is never fully satisfied. The Dalai Lama, who must be celibate given his position, was asked if he was ever attracted to women. His response was that when this temptation came, he pictured them as corpses.[8] This is the grand Buddhist "No!" pronounced on all existence, spare Nirvana. Contrast this with the biblical condemnation of lust but its commendation of sexual enjoyment within marriage (Mt 5:27-32; 1 Cor 7; Song of Songs).

This may surprise some readers, given the recent advocacy of Buddhism—or "Buddhism lite"—as a method or even a science of stilling the mind and finding inner peace. More than a cottage industry has sprung up around mindfulness, and it is being advocated broadly—for fire departments, for addiction recovery, and for use in behavioral health units. Some irreligious philosophers and others commend "Buddhism," but dispense with karma, reincarnation, Nirvana, and even the doctrine of no-self,

---

brings people into the Pure Land, a kind of antechamber to Nirvana. See Corduan, *Neighboring Faiths*, 318-49.

[8]James A. Beverley, "Hollywood's Idol," *Christianity Today*, June 11, 2001, www .christianitytoday.com/ct/2001/june11/15.64.html.

which is fundamental to the dharma. The bestselling *Why Buddhism Is True*, by Robert Wright, follows this odd and awkward path, which is akin to saying that Christianity is true, but its doctrines of the incarnation or heaven and hell are false or unimportant.[9] Even the "new atheist" Sam Harris has written a book called *Waking Up*, in which he advocates Buddhist practices to find meaning in a godless world.[10] While Buddhism is atheistic in origin, it affirms an objectively sacred reality (Nirvana) that Harris rejects as a full-on secularist.

Buddhism and Badness

Buddhism is an ancient and globally practiced religion, which has generated significant philosophical reflection on the nature of the self, suffering, and consciousness in general. It is a religion that has emphasized the virtue of compassion. There is much to explore and fathom. However, our focus will be on Buddhism's understanding of what's wrong with the world—suffering and its causes. This will be contrasted with the Christian view. Once again, contrast is the mother of clarity.

For Buddhism, what's wrong with the world is the world itself. A good creation did not fall into sin, as the Bible teaches (Gen 3). The First Noble Truth is *Life is suffering*. This is offered as more of a definition than a general description. Suffering in our weary and wounded world is undeniable. Even those who think that good and evil are nothing but the result of a lower form of consciousness (such as nondualists, Christian Scientists,

---

[9]See Douglas Groothuis, "Why Buddhism Is Not True," review of *Why Buddhism Is True: The Science and Philosophy of Meditation and Enlightenment*, by Robert Wright, *Christian Research Journal*, April 29, 2019, www.equip.org/article/why-buddhism -is-not-true-review-of-why-buddhism-is-true-the-science-and-philosophy-of-meditation -and-enlightenment.

[10]Sam Harris, *Waking Up: A Guide to Spirituality Without Religion* (New York: Simon and Schuster, 2015).

and many New Agers) cannot deny that people experience suffering in a sadly broad variety of forms, from minor irritants to major traumas, such as chronic illness, fatal illness, physical incapacities, relational breakdowns, social injustices, crime, war, ad nauseam.

To show how radical and non-Western the Buddhist idea of life and suffering is, consider the contrast with the philosophy of utilitarianism, as developed by Jeremy Bentham (1748–1832) and John Stuart Mill (1806–1873). These philosophers were social reformers who tried to reformulate ethics on the basis of the subjective state of happiness. The value to be conserved and furthered was happiness. Their theory of the good was to maximize as much pleasure for as many people (and all sentient beings) as possible over the long haul.

Bentham was an atheist, and Mill held a form of theism but not Christianity. There is much wrong with their theory, given its attenuated concept of value (hedonism) and much else, but they affirmed that human thriving was possible and should be encouraged through the right moral principles and social policies. As such, they were optimistic about the human prospect and so were influenced by a Christian view of progress and human betterment, their personal religious beliefs notwithstanding.

What a contrast this is from Buddhism, which is uninterested in maximizing pleasure over against suffering for social betterment! *Life is suffering*, and the final answer is not social improvement for a happier life for more people but flight from this life entirely through attaining Nirvana. In fact, craving happiness, for the Buddhist, is the cause of suffering so it must be extinguished for release to occur. Release is not found in the satisfaction that happiness brings but in the renouncing of hedonic satisfaction entirely.

JESUS AND BUDDHA ON LIFE, DEATH, AND SALVATION

From that perhaps unexpected comparison of Buddhism and utilitarianism, we move to the teachings of Jesus compared to Buddha concerning suffering and spiritual liberation. Jesus, unlike Buddha, taught within a metaphysically rich worldview. Buddha did not lack a metaphysic, but he deemed some philosophical questions to be unnecessary and even distracting. These included whether the world began to exist or had always existed, whether the world was finite or infinite, whether body and soul were separate, and whether the enlightened one continued to exist when attaining Nirvana. Since Buddha never claimed to be a prophet from God, divine revelation was not available. His metaphysics would thus be hampered from the beginning.

While Buddha claimed not to answer the question of the origin or nonorigin of the universe, Buddhist teaching assumes the eternality of the universe since it denies there is a Creator. However, the other matters were not pertinent to enlightenment, according to Buddha. If you are shot with a burning arrow, he taught, you need to pull it out, not worry about who shot it or other contingencies. It causes suffering so it must be extracted. Similarly, since *Life is suffering*, the suffering must be extracted, and extraneous matters must not obfuscate the cause.

Jesus, on the other hand, had no such metaphysical reticence. He taught that right beliefs about a certain class of metaphysical issues were vital for spiritual liberation and spiritual living, especially beliefs about him personally. In Jesus' evening conversation with Nicodemus, he repeatedly spoke for spiritual rebirth to come through proper recognition of Jesus himself (Jn 3:1-21). For example, "For God so loved the world that he gave his one and only Son, that whoever believes in him shall not perish but have eternal life" (Jn 3:16). Jesus later says that "whoever lives by the truth comes into the light" (Jn 3:21). Living by the truth requires correct beliefs and proper actions in light of those beliefs.

As a Jewish monotheist, Jesus believed that a personal and perfect God created the world and structured it morally (Mt 19:1-6). He taught his disciples to pray beginning with "our Father in heaven," so confident was he that the object of prayer was both personal and parental (Mt 6:9-13). Since Jesus was a monotheist, he believed that the world was finite, not infinite, since only God is infinite (meaning all-good and all-powerful).[11] The universe had a beginning in time and was under God's authority. (Science and philosophy have confirmed that the universe had a beginning a finite time ago.)[12]

On the nature of humanity, Jesus was not bashful to proclaim: "Do not be afraid of those who kill the body but cannot kill the soul. Rather, be afraid of the One who can destroy both soul and body in hell" (Mt 10:28). This was no idle speculation but a matter of eternal consequence. The body and the soul make up the human person; they are distinct and separable. Jesus promised the thief on the cross next to him that "today" they would be together in paradise (Lk 23:43). Jesus then prayed, "Into your hands, I commit my spirit" (Lk 23:46). Matthew says that Jesus "gave up his spirit" when he died from crucifixion (Mt 27:50). Jesus' teaching has force because he affirmed the existence of eternal life after death and the final judgment by a holy God of both one's body and one's soul that ensues after one's death (Mt 7:15-27; 25:31-46; Jn 5:16-30).

---

[11]Neither Jesus nor his disciples nor the religious establishment of that day would use abstract philosophical words such as *finite* or *infinite*, but the concepts are present nonetheless.

[12]See Douglas Groothuis, "The Cosmological Argument: A Cause for the Cosmos," in *Christian Apologetics: A Comprehensive Case for Biblical Faith*, 2nd ed. (Downers Grove, IL: IVP Academic, 2022).

Jesus' body of teaching and his manner of living evinced a worldview infinitely distant from that of Buddha. While they affirmed similar moral teachings, their sense of life, death, and salvation was at loggerheads with each other and cannot be reconciled. Let us take suffering as our port of entry into their respective metaphysics.

For Buddha, life was suffused with suffering, which was caused by craving. Craving must be eliminated through a disciplined life. Then, liberation (Nirvana) was possible. Jesus, affirming the Hebrew Bible, believed that life was not suffering.[13] The universe was created good by a good God (Gen 1–2). After God created humans in his image and likeness on the sixth day, he deemed his whole work "very good" and then rested cosmically content on the seventh day, the sabbath. Suffering came about when our first parents disobeyed God, made themselves the center of the world, and were thus banished from the garden and relocated into a world under the curses of the fall (Gen 3). This fallen condition, which Ecclesiastes calls "life under the sun" (e.g., Eccl 2:17), has been the lot of humanity ever since. The doctrine of original sin does not mean that humans were brought into the world as defective but that humanity is tainted deeply by sin ever since the first sin against God. Jesus found the root of our problems in ourselves.

> What comes out of a person is what defiles them. For it is from within, out of a person's heart, that evil thoughts come— sexual immorality, theft, murder, adultery, greed, malice, deceit, lewdness, envy, slander, arrogance and folly. All these evils come from inside and defile a person. (Mk 7:20-23)

---

[13]Jesus' endorsement of the Hebrew Bible is found throughout the tenor of his teachings and specifically in Matthew 5:17-20 and John 10:33. For more on this, see Groothuis, *Christian Apologetics*, 507-9.

All these vices stem from covetousness or lust—desire gone bad through self-centeredness. But desire in itself is not wrong, according to Jesus. In fact, he says, "Blessed are those who hunger and thirst for righteousness, for they will be filled" (Mt 5:6). Disordered desires stem from sin and generate more sin.

As David confessed to his Lord, "Surely I was sinful at birth, / sinful from the time my mother conceived me" (Ps 51:5). Paul puts this into a theological perspective when he writes, "Sin entered the world through one man, and death through sin, and in this way death came to all people, because all sinned" (Rom 5:12).

The relationship of sin to suffering in Christianity is radically different from the relationship of karma and suffering in Buddhism. According to the Bible, there would be no human suffering without sin. People would have loved God and their neighbor in proper proportion—God receiving love through worship and neighbor receiving love due a fellow creature. Sin is a relational break between Creator and creature that results in disordered heart and life. As Francis Schaeffer put it, "Let us remember that the Fall resulted in division not only between God and man, and man and man, but between man and himself."[14] These three relationships are all damaged by the fall, and all three need to be restored through the agency of Jesus Christ as Lord and Savior.

For Buddhism, *Life is suffering.* There is no fall from an original created goodness into suffering. Humans are not made in the image of God since there is no God. Being human and suffering are conterminous. Suffering is integral and inexorable to all of existence, spare Nirvana. Karma and rebirth occur, not because of any relational breakdown between creature and Creator but

---

[14]Francis A. Schaeffer, *The God Who Is There* (Downers Grove, IL: InterVarsity Press, 1998), 127, Kindle.

because they are fueled by the craving for existence, the desire to satisfy a self that does not really exist. One is released from karma only through the self-effort required to attain Nirvana. (It is an open question to me whether desiring a state without desire is philosophically coherent. As long as one desires, one cannot achieve Nirvana. Therefore, one must strive for a state of no striving, a kind of neutrality to existence.[15]) Further, karma is an automatic cosmic process, not a punishment by God. Nor is there any love or grace in karma; it is a heartless and invariable cosmic system—and one from which to escape as soon as possible.

For Buddhism, earthly life is literally hopeless. There is no possible satisfaction of desire here, and there is no possibility for the wheel of samsara to be reformed, renewed, or resurrected. It must be escaped. Nirvana is the only hope, and it is a state without desire; the combustion of human desire, which causes suffering, has been snuffed out forever. It is not a state in which the deepest human longings have been fulfilled but one in which they have all been extinguished. What remains is difficult to state at all. Buddhists are reluctant to say much about the nature of Nirvana, beyond what Buddha himself said. Speaking of Nirvana, Buddha said to his disciples:

> O bhikkhus, there is the unborn, ungrown, and uncondi-
> tioned. Were there not the unborn, ungrown, and uncon-
> ditioned, there would be no escape for the born, grown,
> and conditioned. Since there is the unborn, ungrown, and
> unconditioned, so there is escape for the born, grown,
> and conditioned.[16]

---

[15]David L. Johnson, *A Reasoned Look at Asian Religions* (Minneapolis: Bethany Books, 1985), 131-32, believes the quest for Nirvana is incoherent. Gruzalski, "The Possibility of Liberation," defends it as coherent.

[16]Walpola Rahula, *What the Buddha Taught*, rev. and enl. ed. with texts from Suttas and Dhammapada (New York: Grove, 1974), 69, Kindle.

Gruzalski claims that Buddha was an "ineffabilist" in that Nirvana could not be described in words, and this resonates with Buddhist tradition.[17] If so, Buddhism is subject to the same kinds of problems raised in our chapters on Hinduism and Daoism. If the ultimate reality is beyond coherent description (whether Brahman or Dao or Nirvana), we can have little confidence in our ability to make it intelligible or even desirable.[18]

The ultimate solution to suffering for the Buddhist is Nirvana. Yet, for those not there, some relief is offered in the teaching of impermanence (*anicca*). The self is not an enduring substance but a collection of impermanent states. Nature lacks substance as well; it is not a system of stable entities and fixed relationships that ensure the maintenance of fixed beings, such as humans, animals, and trees. Reality is, rather, a collection of instances or points that arise and disappear almost instantly. This is known as the doctrine of dependent origination.

But what can be done in the face of suffering before achieving Nirvana? What can Buddhism offer for times of extreme distress given its worldview? Let us consider two accounts. The first is given by Os Guinness and has resonated with me as I have taught on Buddhism for several decades:

> The Japanese poet, Issa (1762–1826), [was] perhaps the best loved of all Haiku poets because of the humanness of his writing. His own life was very sad. All five of his children died before he was thirty, and then his young wife died. After one of those deaths he went to a Zen master and asked him for an explanation for such suffering. The master reminded him that the world was dew. Just as the sun rises and the dew evaporates, so on the wheel of suffering sorrow

---

[17]Gruzalski, *On the Buddha*, 27-30.
[18]This problem is treated in more detail in the following chapter on Daoism.

is transient, life is transient, man is transient. Involvement in the passion of grief and mourning speaks of a failure to transcend the momentum of selfish egoism. Here was his religious philosophical answer, but on returning home Issa wrote a poem which translated literally runs:

> This Dewdrop World—
> a dewdrop world it is, and still,
> although it is. . . .

Or more simply,

> The world is dew—
> The world is dew—
> And yet,
> And yet . . .[19]

The Zen master was true to Buddha and Buddhism. "Life is dew" means that it is impermanent; nothing has substance; reality is a collection of arising and disappearing instances that last only a moment. Thus, do not grieve. That is what life is (outside of Nirvana). It could be nothing more. But while the Zen master was true to Buddha and Buddhism, he was false to the reality of the wounded human heart "under the sun." Issa could not find refuge in the Buddha or his teachings since it contradicted his deepest longings and need to lament the loss of his beloved family members.

> The world is dew—
> The world is dew—
> And yet,
> And yet . . .

---

[19]Os Guinness, *The Dust of Death: The Sixties Counterculture and How It Changed America Forever* (Downers Grove, IL: InterVarsity Press, 2020), 196, Kindle.

Another account takes up suffering, but this one is contained in Buddhist Scripture. A young woman named Gotami was grieving terribly over the death of her young son, whom she carried from house to house looking for medicine. Most mocked her, but one man said to go to the Buddha. He neither laughed at her nor told her that her son was dead nor taught about impermanence. Instead, he said she had done well to come to him. He then told her to canvass her entire city and fetch grains of mustard seed from every household in which no one had died and to bring those to Buddha. She did so, and found no household was death free.

When she realized that the Buddha out of compassion had wanted her to see the widespread fact of death, she had her son cremated, said goodbye to him, and said, "Dear little son, . . . I thought that you alone had been overtaken by this thing which men call death. But you are not the only one death has overtaken. This is a law common to all mankind." She then found the Buddha, who asked her if she had any mustard seeds from her search; she said she was finished looking for medicine and asked to go to him for refuge.[20]

Unlike poor Issa, Gotami accepted death as a universal condition and inevitable. She found refuge in the Buddha. Whether this story is historical or not, it underscores the Buddhist teaching that "life is dew," *Life is suffering*, and death is universal since everything is impermanent.

Buddhism has no holiday approximating Easter (better called Resurrection Day), for reasons that should be clear. But many Easter sermons recount what happened when Jesus was summoned to the tomb of his friend Lazarus as recorded in John 11. This account throws Jesus and Buddha into clear relief.

---

[20]This is recounted in Gruzalski, *On the Buddha*, 39-40. He cites *The Anguttar Commentary*: 225-27.

Jesus was called by the sisters of Lazarus, Mary and Martha, to attend to Lazarus because he was ill. Jesus responded by saying, "This sickness will not end in death. No, it is for God's glory so that God's Son may be glorified through it" (Jn 11:4). But Jesus stayed where he was for two days. Despite facing opposition from the Jewish leadership, Jesus went back to Judea. He said to his disciples, "Lazarus is dead, and for your sake I am glad I was not there, so that you may believe. But let us go to him" (Jn 11:14-15). When Jesus reached Bethany, he learned that Lazarus had been in a tomb for four days. Martha went out to meet Jesus before he entered her village. Jesus' conversation with Martha needs to be recounted.

> "Lord," Martha said to Jesus, "if you had been here, my brother would not have died. But I know that even now God will give you whatever you ask."
>
> Jesus said to her, "Your brother will rise again."
>
> Martha answered, "I know he will rise again in the resurrection at the last day."
>
> Jesus said to her, "I am the resurrection and the life. The one who believes in me will live, even though they die; and whoever lives by believing in me will never die. Do you believe this?"
>
> "Yes, Lord," she replied, "I believe that you are the Messiah, the Son of God, who is to come into the world."
> (Jn 11:21-27)

But despite Martha's great confession of faith (one of the most forceful in the Gospels before the resurrection), her brother Lazarus was still dead and lying in his tomb; and Jesus could have prevented it by coming sooner to heal him, as he had healed so many before that. When Mary found that her sister Martha had been talking to Jesus, she quickly went to meet him.

Throwing herself at his feet, she cried, "Lord, if you had been here, my brother would not have died" (Jn 11:32). What happens next dramatically discloses Jesus' heart and his power.

> When Jesus saw [Martha] weeping, and the Jews who had come along with her also weeping, he was deeply moved in spirit and troubled. "Where have you laid him?" he asked.
> "Come and see, Lord," they replied.
> Jesus wept. (Jn 11:33-35)

Lest we read past these verses too quickly, consider the phrase that Jesus was "deeply moved in his spirit and troubled." As B. B. Warfield noted in his classic essay, "The Emotional Life of Our Lord," these words indicate a profound anger in the face of death and bereavement.

> What John tells us, in point of fact, is that Jesus approached the grave of Lazarus, in a state, not of uncontrollable grief, but of irrepressible anger. He did respond to the spectacle of human sorrow abandoning itself to its unrestrained expression, with quiet, sympathetic tears: "Jesus wept" (verse 36). But the emotion which tore his breast and clamored for utterance was just rage. The expression even of this rage, however, was strongly curbed.[21]

Jesus did not rage out of control, but he was inwardly repulsed and incensed by the death that had invaded his Father's world through sin. After raging, he wept, and felt no shame.

Jesus was indignant over suffering and death. He let himself suffer by weeping with the others who wept. Remarkably, he responded this way even knowing what would happen next.

---

[21]B. B. Warfield, "The Emotional Life of Our Lord," excerpt from *The Person and Work of Christ* (Phillipsburg, NJ: P&R, 1989), 93-145, accessed January 4, 2023, www.monergism .com/thethreshold/articles/onsite/emotionallife.html.

Jesus, once more deeply moved, came to the tomb. It was a cave with a stone laid across the entrance. "Take away the stone," he said.

"But, Lord," said Martha, the sister of the dead man, "by this time there is a bad odor, for he has been there four days."

Then Jesus said, "Did I not tell you that if you believe, you will see the glory of God?"

So they took away the stone. Then Jesus looked up and said, "Father, I thank you that you have heard me. I knew that you always hear me, but I said this for the benefit of the people standing here, that they may believe that you sent me."

When he had said this, Jesus called in a loud voice, "Lazarus, come out!" The dead man came out, his hands and feet wrapped with strips of linen, and a cloth around his face.

Jesus said to them, "Take off the grave clothes and let him go." (Jn 11:38-44)

The story ends here, with no account of the surprise and joy that must have been felt by those who thought their brother and friend was dead. For Jesus, this resurrection looked ahead to his own resurrection and to the resurrection of the dead at the end of history: "I am the resurrection and the life," he affirmed.

SUFFERING: BUDDHA AND JESUS

According to the Bible, no one suffered as terribly as Jesus did on the cross. Suffering stems from sin, but Jesus, the Savior, came to earth to atone for sin through his own sinless offering of himself as a substitute on our behalf. On the cross, he cried out a lament from Psalm 22:

"About three in the afternoon Jesus cried out in a loud voice, *"Eli, Eli, lema sabachthani?"* (which means "My God, my God, why have you forsaken me?"). (Mt 27:46)

Jesus lamented the effects of sin in the death of his friend Lazarus but still offers resurrection for today and tomorrow. For Buddha, suffering is overcome only through what can only be called dehumanization: one must be stripped of all longing for a better world, for a healed body, for restored relationships, for balm for a broken earth. For Jesus, suffering was a fact to overcome. For Buddha, suffering was life itself, and only the absolute denial of life as we know it in Nirvana could be the cure.[22] But it seems that the cure kills the patient. Speaking from another realm, Jesus affirmed, "The thief comes only to steal and kill and destroy; I have come that they may have life, and have it to the full" (Jn 10:10).

---

[22]For more on the philosophical comparisons between Christianity and Buddhism, see Keith Yandell and Harold Netland, *Buddhism: A Christian Exploration and Appraisal* (Downers Grove, IL: IVP Academic, 2008), especially 105-211. See also Johnson, *Reasoned Look*, 117-43.

- five -

DAOISM

*"The Dao that can be spoken
is not the eternal Dao."*

T he question whether we can know ultimate reality is really the ultimate question. By ultimate reality, I mean the prime reality or the really real, that which is the fundamental fact to which all else relates. This could be God (personal or impersonal), the gods, or the physical cosmos.[1] How we answer it—or how we ignore it—determines who we are and how we live. The ultimate reality should be our ultimate concern, and our ultimate concern should match the ultimate reality.[2] If the apex of reality is within our apprehension, then it behooves us to know it and live in terms of it. The ancient Hebrews believed that God had spoken his name and revealed his being to his people and that this was the foundation for their lives as

---

[1] This is the first of seven worldview questions in James W. Sire's modern classic, *The Universe Next Door: A Basic Worldview Catalog*, 5th ed. (Downers Grove, IL: IVP Academic, 2009), 22.

[2] Some readers may think of theologian Paul Tillich's idea of "ultimate concern" here, but that is not my intent since I take issue with how he develops this idea. See Paul Tillich, *Systematic Theology*, 3 vols. in 1 (Chicago: University of Chicago Press, 1967), 12-14.

individuals and as a people. Christianity teaches that God has made himself known in many ways, but preeminently through his Son, Jesus Christ (Jn 1:1-18; Heb 1:3-4). Islam claims that the Qur'an is God's final revelation. Other religions demur. Daoism is one of them.

Relatively speaking, there are few Daoists (or Taoists) worldwide or in the United States.[3] Perhaps only thirty thousand would identify as such in America.[4] Despite all my discussions about other faiths and with members of other faiths, I have never met anyone who identified as Daoist, although a Daoist priest spoke at the University of Oregon when I attended there in 1977. Daoism is not a missionary religion, as are Christianity, Islam, and Buddhism. Nevertheless, Daoism is an ancient and venerable religious tradition and is one of the three classic religious teachings of China, along with Confucianism and neo-Confucianism. Daoists can be found in many Far Eastern countries, such as China, Taiwan, Hong Kong, and Singapore; estimates of total adherents varies wildly. According to WorldAtlas.com, "There could be as many as 173 million Taoists globally or as little as 12 million."[5]

Daoism appeals to those who yearn to live in harmony with the deepest principles of the universe. Those who want to "go with the flow" resonate with Daoism, as do those who shun convention and formality in favor of spontaneity and naturalness. Daoism inspired the Beat vagabond and literary nomad Jack Kerouac (1922–1969) to famously go "on the road,"

---

[3]Until a few decades ago, the preferred spelling was *Taoist*. More recently *Daoist* is common so I will use it.

[4]"American Daoism in the 21st Century," *The Pluralism Project*, Harvard University, 2020, accessed January 4, 2023, https://hwpi.harvard.edu/files/pluralism/files/american _daoism_in_the_21st_century_1.pdf.

[5]"Taoism," *WorldAtlas*, accessed January 4, 2023, www.worldatlas.com/articles/taoism .html.

and he carried a copy of the *Daodejing* (or *Tao Te Ching*) in his back pocket.[6]

Although few call themselves Daoists, not a few hold Daoist ideas. It would be unusual to find a large bookstore lacking copies of the *Daodejing*, the central text of Daoism. It is likewise common to find many books with *Tao* in the title, such as *The Tao of Physics* or the popular *The Tao of Pooh* or even *The Tao of Jesus*. The *Daodejing* is one of the most translated books in history, ranking behind the Bible. Moreover, the famous statement *The Dao that can be spoken is not the eternal Dao*[7] encapsulates a distinctive approach to the sacred, which is shared in various ways by Eastern religions as a whole, especially Hinduism and Buddhism. That idea is that the ultimate reality lies beyond the reach of words and thoughts. Before exploring that idea, we consider the fundamentals of Daoism.

LAOZI AND DAOISM

Although Daoism is most known for a text written by its purported Chinese founder, Laozi (or Lao Tzu [b. 604 BC]), little is known about him. His name means "old sage." The religion is not named after him, as in Buddhism, Christianity, or Zoroastrianism.[8] The events in Laozi's life are rather incidental to the message he left since he is deemed a sage, not a prophet (like Moses or Muhammad), much less an incarnation (Christ) or

---

[6]Jack Kerouac chronicled his wanderings in both *On the Road* (New York: Viking, 1957) and *The Dharma Bums* (New York: Viking, 1958). Mark Sayers explores the American penchant for road trips as a way of life in *The Road Trip That Changed the World* (Chicago: Moody, 2012).

[7]This has been translated in several ways. Literally, it reads, "The Dao that can be Daoed is not the eternal Dao," thus muddling the waters even more. However, most translations emphasize the unspeakability of the Dao, so I use that rendering here.

[8]Islam has been called Muhammedanism, but Muslims insist on Islam, which means submission to God. Muhammad is the final prophet but not the center of worship. Thus, Muhammedanism is seldom used today. See my chapter on Islam in this volume.

even an avatar (Krishna). A sage may be understood supernaturally or nonsupernaturally. The New Testament takes Jesus to be a sage (Mk 6:2), but it claims that his wisdom came from God.[9] Sages, such as Laozi and Buddha, have purportedly found wisdom without aid of God or the supernatural.

Legend has it that Laozi was born at the age of seventy-two, a feat that would win him an entry in *Guinness World Records*. This mind-boggling claim is that "anyone as wise as this man could not possibly have been born as a squalling infant. Instead, he came into the world possessing white hair and the ability to speak."[10] History has preserved little about Laozi beyond the likelihood that he was a contemporary of Confucius and that he left a text that became the primary text of Daoism. Some doubt his very existence. But most think that Laozi lived a quiet life as an archivist at the court of a nobleman and gathered a few disciples. He decided to leave China to travel west. When he reached the western boundary of China, Laozi was greeted by a gatekeeper at the border who demanded that he write down his wisdom for posterity before he would let him through. The sage complied, and in one sitting wrote the short book *Daodejing* (sometimes called *The Laozi*), which means, "the way and its power." For Daoism, the book is more important than the man.

The eponymous *Zhuangzi* (or *Chuang-tzu)* came later and develops the themes of the *Daodejing*. This is the second central text of Daoism, and it too agrees that the Dao is beyond words. Scholars debate the roles that Laozi and Chuang-tzu had in the texts that bear their names since each book seems to have varied

---

[9]Ben Witherington III, *Jesus the Sage: The Pilgrimage of Wisdom* (Minneapolis: Fortress, 2000).

[10]Winfried Corduan, *Neighboring Faiths*, 2nd ed. (Downers Grove, IL: IVP Academic, 2012), 398, Kindle.

textually over hundreds of years. Both are probably collaborative efforts, whose origins recede into misty antiquity.

Daoism as a worldview is difficult to summarize, but it affirms that reality is ultimately unified through a controlling principle, the Dao, although it manifests through the opposites of yin and yang. Thus, it could be called a dipolar monism and not a strict dualism. The Dao is more of an impersonal principle than a personal being; it gives form and shape to nature, but it can only be discerned by transcending the conventions of society, even its moral codes. The Daoist returns to "the uncarved block" of original nature—which is the Dao itself—and forsakes the artificial in favor of the organic. Instead of taking charge and molding the world into one's egotistic image, one should, rather, take the way of nonaction, or *wu-wei*. Many of the aphorisms of the *Daodejing* speak to this:

Man was not made to blow out air
He was made to sit quietly and find the truth within.[11]

Daoism shuns the moralism of Confucianism and teaches that moral rules arise when people and governments get out of sync with the Dao, thus tending toward a naturalistic amoralism.[12] After all, the Dao does not speak, and so does not command, reward, or punish.

Daoism did not graduate from philosophy to religion until long after Laozi's death. It later "became the undergirding for endeavors in alchemy and in the search for immortality. Then, it eventually evolved personal gods and religious rituals."[13] These magical and metaphysical layers seem out of character from the

---

[11]Lao Tzu, *Tao Te Ching*, trans. Jonathan Star (New York: Tarcher/Penguin, 2001), 6, Kindle.

[12]See John M. Koller, *Oriental Philosophies* (New York: Charles Scribner's and Sons, 1970), 238-39.

[13]Corduan, *Neighboring Faiths*, 401, Kindle.

aphoristic ruminations on "the way and its power," but its current form bears similarities to other religions. Much later, Daoist ideas were synthesized with the teachings of the Buddha to produce Zen Buddhism, an iconoclastic and direct-experience-oriented variant of Buddhism, which has been popular in the West.[14] But our concern is with this much-translated and long-pondered book, the *Daodejing*.

THE DAODEJING

This a collection of eighty-one short sayings, usually divided into two sections. Printings usually put only a few sentences on each page, giving the sense that one should not read too quickly. The space surrounding the text also plays into the Daoist idea that emptiness is just as important as form, nonbeing as important as being. Without the white space, there would be no dark lettering or inscription. An image that might help to explain its sentiments is the hub of the wheel (hollow-nothing), which supports the spokes (being).[15] John Minford, one of the myriad translators of *Daodejing*, writes, "The book proceeds in an intuitive, poetic, non-logical, zigzag, often repetitive, and sometimes incoherent fashion."[16] Both the Christian philosopher Stuart Hackett[17] and the atheist philosopher Walter Kauffmann[18] have praised its charming literary qualities, although neither was a Daoist. Much of the book seems to have been written for

---

[14]See D. T. Suzuki, *An Introduction to Zen Buddhism* (New York: Grove, 1994). For a critique of Zen, see Lit-sen Chang, *Zen-Existentialism: The Spiritual Decline of the West* (1969; rep., Eugene, OR: Wipf and Stock, 2011).

[15]Lao Tzu, *Tao Te Ching*, 38. Chap. 11 addresses this.

[16]John Minford, trans., introduction to *Tao Te Ching*, by Lao Tzu (New York: Viking, 2018), xxii.

[17]Stuart C. Hackett, *Oriental Philosophy: A Westerner's Guide to Eastern Thought* (Madison: University of Wisconsin Press, 1979), 56.

[18]Walter Kaufmann, *Religions in Four Dimensions* (New York: Reader's Digest Press, 1977), 339.

political rulers, and its general political tenor is (to use our phrase) libertarian. Spontaneity should be given ample place in governing:

> The more restrictions, the more poverty
> The more weapons, the more fear in the land
> The more cleverness, the more strange events
> The more laws, the more lawbreakers[19]

But our concern is more about epistemology than civil government, although the two are related.

WHAT CANNOT BE SPOKEN

What of this statement *The Dao that can be spoken is not the eternal Dao*, which begins the book? It has been translated in several ways, but all I have seen retain the idea of the Dao's ineffability—the Dao cannot be described in words since it transcends rational thought. The statement seems profound at first sight since the eternal principle of existence could not be a matter of cheap talk, bull sessions in university dorms, tweets, or Instagram posts. It must be deeper. But the statement needs to be analyzed since nonsense and illogic sometimes wear the mystical robes of mystery.

The statement certainly means that, according to Corduan, "the Dao itself lies beyond human categorization in terms of language and rational thought. Trying to put its nature into words produces a mere imitation that does not convey the reality of the Dao."[20] Koller argues that the Dao cannot be named because it is without "divisions, distinctions, or characteristics. It is unified, like an uncarved block."[21] It cannot be named since "it is the

---

[19]Lao Tzu, *Tao Te Ching*, 74.
[20]Corduan, *Neighboring Faiths*, 399, Kindle.
[21]Koller, *Oriental Philosophies*, 236.

very source of names and descriptions." Thus, Dao is really "a non-name." It is "that from which being and non-being proceed."[22] But there is no obvious reason why "the very source of names and descriptions" should lack a name or description, especially if we assume that like causes like or, to use Descartes's more refined causal principle:

> Now it is indeed evident by the light of nature that there must be at least as much [reality] in the efficient and total cause as there is in the effect of that same cause. For whence, I ask, could an effect get its reality, if not from its cause? And how could the cause give that reality to the effect, unless it also possessed that reality? Hence it follows that something cannot come into being out of nothing, and also that what is more perfect (that is, what contains in itself more reality) cannot come into being from what is less perfect.[23]

Moreover, if the Dao is the ultimate reality and is "unified, like an uncarved block," it cannot explain the diversity of things (or particulars) that exist in nature: trees, rocks, mountains, flowers, humans, and the like. Diversity must be either denied as illusion or remain unexplained and absurd.

In one way, *The Dao that can be spoken is not the eternal Dao* is transparently true. A statement about the Dao is not the same as the Dao itself. A statement about my dog Sunny—"Sunny is a goldendoodle"—is not the same as Sunny, the goldendoodle, himself. The reference ("Sunny") is not the same as the referent (Sunny). That point is trivial, though; and a statement that merely illustrates it is not worth enshrining in the hall of spiritual fame.

---

[22]Koller, *Oriental Philosophies*, 236. He repeats this point several times, giving a Daoist account of the Dao in his words.

[23]René Descartes, *Discourse on Method and Meditations on First Philosophy*, trans. Donald A. Cress, 4th ed. (Indianapolis: Hackett, 1998), 73, Kindle.

(However, a statement can refer to itself, such as "This statement is in English," which is true, or "This statement is in French," which is false.)

"The Dao" means, roughly, the way of nature and the right way of life. But as Corduan notes, the "basic notion of Dao, consisting of the right balance between yin and yang, is the property of all of Chinese thought in all of its schools, though subject to the schools' particular interpretations."[24] Throughout the *Daodejing*, the Dao is described in prose-poetic sentences. It breaks new ground for Chinese philosophy by asserting that the complementary elements of yin and yang place them into a monistic whole, the Dao.[25]

Despite its supposed ineffability, certain qualities are attributed to the Dao and certain qualities are withheld from it. Koller called it "unified," which is different from "diversified." Such attribution is not surprising since to discuss anything coherently, some qualities must be affixed and some withheld. Thus, something has, after all, been spoken of about "the eternal Dao," appearances to the contrary. The Dao is called "eternal." Thus, the adjective *eternal* is ascribed to the noun, *Dao*. Therefore, the Dao must not be non-eternal or temporal. Nor is the "eternal Dao" another incidental fact of nature, such as, "Fireweed appears in Willow, Alaska, in July but soon dies." Rather, "the eternal" is limitless in both directions of time, past and future—unlike fireweed. The Dao is not identical to any one thing in nature, say a bear or a mosquito. It is more than that, but what exactly?

Alan Watts (1915–1973), the Episcopalian priest who became a prominent and eloquent exponent of Eastern religion for the

---

[24]Corduan, *Neighboring Faiths*, 393-94, Kindle.
[25]See Koller, *Oriental Philosophies*, 236.

West, called Daoism "the watercourse way."[26] The word "water" appears frequently in the Dao. This should not be confused with another aquatic philosophy, that of the pre-Socratic philosopher Thales of Miletus, who concluded that the one material substance from which all came was water or moisture. The Dao is not literally water or any material thing or substance, even in a rarefied or variable form. Water is a metaphor, not a metaphysic. The way of water is the way of least resistance. Water will find the lowest point available; it will seep wherever it finds passage; it will work slowly but surely in its way:

> The Best is like Water.
> Water Benefits the Myriad Things.
> Water does not Contend.
> It abides in that
> Which the Multitude abhor.
> It is close to the Tao.[27]

The great Christian writer C. S. Lewis wrote of the Tao. In *The Abolition of Man*, a book defending objective moral value, he writes of the various religions and philosophies that have agreed that there is an irreducible moral good beyond the contingencies of culture, the urges of instinct, and personal preference. He writes, "This conception in all its forms, Platonic, Aristotelian, Stoic, Christian, and Oriental alike, I shall henceforth refer to for brevity simply as 'the Tao.'"[28] Earlier in the book he explained the original concept of "the Tao."

---

[26]Alan Watts, with Al Chung-liang Huang, *Tao: The Watercourse Way* (New York: Pantheon, 1975). I am not endorsing Watt's worldview, which was pantheistic. Much of what he believed is addressed in the chapter "You Are That" in this book. For a critique of Watt's worldview, see David K. Clark, *The Pantheism of Alan Watts* (Downers Grove, IL: InterVarsity Press, 1977).

[27]Lao Tzu, *Tao Te Ching*, 28.

[28]C. S. Lewis, *The Abolition of Man* (New York: HarperOne, 2001), 19, Kindle.

The Chinese also speak of a great thing (the greatest thing) called the Tao. It is the reality beyond all predicates, the abyss that was before the Creator Himself. It is Nature, it is the Way, the Road. It is the Way in which the universe goes on, the Way in which things everlastingly emerge, stilly and tranquilly, into space and time. It is also the Way which every man should tread in imitation of that cosmic and supercosmic progression, conforming all activities to that great exemplar.[29]

Whatever else Lewis says about the Dao is, however, disqualified if it is "the reality beyond all predicates." If so, the Dao cannot serve as the moral foundation for anything since it cannot be described. Lewis's description seems faithful to the Daoist understanding, but the philosophical problem is the Daoist understanding, not Lewis's rendition. To be "beyond all predicates" is to be unknowable since, to know anything, we must identify and believe in some predicate of a subject. I know that my wife, Kathleen, is gentle and kind. The adjectival predicates (*gentle* and *kind*) are attributed to a noun, *Kathleen* (the subject of the predicates). To say that X is "beyond all predicates" is to precisely say nothing about anything. This linguistic act differs from saying you are largely in the dark about something. If I say, "What Sunny did is beyond me," is not to foreclose all predicates as applying to Sunny, but only some of them—those pertaining to why he did something out of character. I know Sunny is a goldendoodle, that he is cute, and more. In 1939, Winston Churchill famously defined Russia as "a riddle, wrapped in a mystery, inside an enigma." Nevertheless, much could still be predicated of Russia—it is a large country, it was once ruled by czars, it was taken over by communism in 1919, and more.

---

[29]Lewis, *Abolition of Man*, 19.

Furthermore, there is, by definition, nothing "before the Creator himself," except "the Creator himself," since the Creator qua Creator creates everything outside of himself.[30] In the Creator's mind are all the plans and patterns for the creation, but that is not independent of God himself but is, rather, in his essence as the one self-existent being. The *Daodejing* refers to the Dao as acting according to its intrinsic nature and dependent on nothing else. But, if so, this differentiates the Dao from the world of changing things and processes. But other passages identify the Dao with the world itself. This is part of the enigmatic nature of the text, but if left as is, it constitutes a contradiction. If so, both statements cannot be true since no contradiction can possibly be true. A charitable interpretation might be that the Dao is transcendent in some ways and immanent in some other ways. The text speaks of the Dao birthing nature and also indwelling nature. This passage may indicate this:

The Tao gave
Birth To the One.
The One gave Birth To the Two.
The Two gave Birth To the Three.
The Three gave
Birth To the
Myriad Things.[31]

The idea of giving birth differs from absolute creation out of nothing, as taught in the monotheistic religions. On this view, God and creation are different in kind, and creation is not an emanation or externalization of God. That idea seems lacking pertaining to the Dao, although it does speak of a Creator in places.

---

[30]Unless the text is thinking of a Creator who uses preexistent and uncreated materials, as in Plato's Demiurge.

[31]Lao Tzu, *Tao Te Ching*, 152.

Consider the contrast of the wordlessness and silence of the Dao with the Old Testament view of God speaking through creation.

The heavens declare the glory of God;
    the skies proclaim the work of his hands.
Day after day they pour forth speech;
    night after night they reveal knowledge.
They have no speech, they use no words;
    no sound is heard from them.
Yet their voice goes out into all the earth,
    their words to the ends of the world. (Ps 19:1-4)

Moreover, the Christian Scriptures depict a God who is Lord over nature, who owns it and rules it with sovereign goodness (Ps 24:1-2). This is antithetical to the Dao, which is a flow or process. Watts says that Daoism knows of no ruler and ruled dichotomy; there is nothing monarchial about the universe.[32] The psalmist, to the contrary, declares:

By the word of the LORD the heavens were made,
    their starry host by the breath of his mouth.
He gathers the waters of the sea into jars;
    he puts the deep into storehouses.
Let all the earth fear the LORD;
    let all the people of the world revere him.
For he spoke, and it came to be;
    he commanded, and it stood firm. (Ps 33:6-9)

It seems that something muffled the voice of creation for Laozi. He heard murmurs but not words.[33] However, he left us words that often murmur.

---

[32]Watts, *Tao*, 35.
[33]On how people suppress the truth of God in creation, see Douglas Groothuis, "Doubt, Skepticism, and the Hiddenness of God," in *Christian Apologetics: A Comprehensive Case for Biblical Faith*, 2nd ed. (Downers Grove, IL: IVP Academic, 2022).

THE LAST WORD

The *Daodejing* presents a Dao that, in the final analysis, cannot be spoken of with clarity or finality. Nor does the Dao itself speak of anything to anyone. However, we can limn some of its meaning from the book's allusive comments. The Dao is not lord over nature; nor does it command humans. It may not be entirely synonymous with nature but somehow pervades nature as an elusive presence and subtle power. One can be out of sync with the Dao, but one cannot sin against it. The Dao's nature can be intuited but not proven; it is more felt than thought. A Chinese commentator, The River Master, said of the Dao,

> The Subtle Color and
> Sound of the Tao cannot be
> Told, they must be absorbed in the
> Simple Calm of Spirit, when
> Emotion and Desire have been Stilled.[34]

If words help understand the Dao at all, they must be poetic, illusive, allusive, gnomic, paradoxical, and enigmatic. Daoism has no systematic theologies. One Daoist writer disclosed the essential problem with the *Daodejing*

> Those who speak Know nothing;
> Those who Know Are silent.
> Those Words, I'm told, Were uttered
> By Lao-tzu.
> If we're to believe
> That he himself Was someone who Knew,
> Why did he end up Writing a Book Of Five Thousand
>   Words?[35]

---

[34]Lao Tzu, *Tao Te Ching*, 48. This commentary is added by the translator and editor of the book.
[35]Lao Tzu, *Tao Te Ching*, 6.

The traditional answer is that he was forced to write his philosophy by the border control agent, referred to earlier. Nevertheless, his words have been preserved, treasured, and interpreted ever since. They are more than a bribe or a ransom price. If so, the first aphorism of the text invalidates all that follows.

This is certainly not true of the Old or New Testaments since God is taken to be a personal, relational, and communicative being. To take but one example, Jesus speaks of those who hear the word of God and are blessed by it to produce an ample crop (Mt 13:23). The beginning of the Gospel of John proclaims that Jesus was the Word of God, who took on flesh for our redemption (John 1:1-14). "[He] has made [the Father] known" (John 1:18).

Of all religions, Daoism is least subject to heresy since it has scarcely any creeds or norms to violate. It is not a system of thought based on a perspicacious written authority. Daoism has sages but no prophets. Laozi hailed the way of water while the prophet Jeremiah had fire in his bones from the living God of judgment and mercy (Jer 20:9). He was given a distinct message from God for the people, a message that demanded a response. But the Dao demands nothing, promises nothing, and does not love or care for humanity since it is more like an impersonal and amoral force than a living, acting, and personal being who marks history with its stamp:

This is
The Mystic Union,
Of Heaven-and-Nature,
To be One With the Tao.
Not to be Loved,
Not to bask
In glory,
Not to suffer From loneliness,

Not to be rejected,
To feel no bitterness,
But to have a
Heart-and-Mind Of Calm and Constancy,
With neither Desire nor Aversion.[36]

Perhaps the strongest of all human desires is to be loved and to love. But that is just what oneness with the Dao forbids. That Daoist statement just given would have shocked the apostle John, who wrote,

> God is love. This is how God showed his love among us: He sent his one and only Son into the world that we might live through him. (1 Jn 4:8-9)

While Viktor Frankl was imprisoned in a concentration camp by the Nazis during World War II, he realized the meaning of love when he was meditating on the face of his absent wife.

> A thought transfixed me: for the first time in my life I saw the truth as it is set into song by so many poets, proclaimed as the final wisdom by so many thinkers. The truth—that love is the ultimate and the highest goal to which man can aspire. Then I grasped the meaning of the greatest secret that human poetry and human thought and belief have to impart: The salvation of man is through love and in love. I understood how a man who has nothing left in this world still may know bliss, be it only for a brief moment, in the contemplation of his beloved. In a position of utter desolation, when man cannot express himself in positive action, when his only achievement may consist in enduring his sufferings in the right way—an honorable way—in such a position man can, through loving contemplation of the

---

[36]Lao Tzu, *Tao Te Ching*, 204-5, emphasis added.

image he carries of his beloved, achieve fulfillment. For the first time in my life I was able to understand the meaning of the words, "The angels are lost in perpetual contemplation of an infinite glory."[37]

The Dao appeals to those who would rather commune with nature than worship God, to those who would rather ponder a ponderous text than seek a sure word from God, to those who would rather resonate with nature than worship its Creator. There are rumors of monotheism in the book as well, but these are confused by pantheistic allusions. However, the Dao lies far from Judaism, Christianity, and Islam—religions that demand worship, obedience, and accountability to revealed truths found in sacred Scriptures. In these religions, God is not mute but has spoken in intelligible language. Thus, as opposed to the Dao, which cannot be spoken, God speaks in the Hebrew Bible, in the New Testament, and supposedly in the Qur'an—a claim I will dispute later in this book.

If God had not spoken clearly, then the Dao is a possibility, if it can survive the logical critique just given. But even if God has spoken, the *Daodejing* does offer some advice about humility and forsaking a harried journey through life. Some of its reflections on silence and accepting one's lot remind me of passages in Ecclesiastes about enjoying the simple things in life (Eccl 5:18-20). Still, these kinds of reflections and admonitions are found in the Bible, along with the promise that God will assist the earnest reader in attaining those ends (2 Tim 2:7).

What truth is gleaned from the Dao of Daoism can be likened to a torn-up book that has only a few sentences on each page.[38]

---

[37]Viktor E. Frankl, *Man's Search for Meaning* (Boston: Beacon, 2006), 37-38, Kindle.

[38]I have modified this a bit from the brilliant illustration given by Francis Schaeffer in *The God Who Is There*, rev. ed., IVP Classics (Downers Grove, IL: InterVarsity Press, 2006), 135-36, Kindle.

There is truth there, but it is only partial, and much is puzzling if not false. The overall meaning is obscured because the narrative is lacking; only fragments remain. However, if the missing parts are discovered and placed properly into the torn-up book, what the reader finds is coherent and informative. Communication from author to reader is restored.

The text in this illustration is what can be gleaned from nature and human nature through observation and reflection (and without the aid of the Bible). Daoism rightly tells us that there is unity and meaning to nature and that the ultimate reality is beyond our grasp (if we are left to ourselves). But the story is partial and thus incomplete, if not wrong in parts. The missing pages in this illustration are the biblical teachings about ultimate reality, the human condition, the way of life, and the means of redemption through Jesus Christ. Francis Schaeffer further explains:

> First, the portions of each page left in the book could never tell what the story was about. Their importance would be as a test to determine whether the pieces found in the attic were the right ones for that book. Second, the man who discovered the matching portions used his reason to show that they fitted the mutilated book. But then, on the level of his whole personality, he enjoyed reading and understanding the complete story of the original pieces and the added portions. This would particularly be the case if the total book opened the way to a restored communication with someone important to the reader.[39]

WE ARE NOT LEFT IN THE DARK

The total book of the Bible does not leave us in the dark or liken God to the way of water in the Daoist sense. The Creator "gave

---

[39]Schaeffer, *God Who Is There*, 136.

the sea its boundary / so the waters would not overstep his command" (Prov 8:29). The Bible claims to reveal how to restore communication between God and human beings through the truth of the gospel. As Jesus retorted to the devil in the wilderness, "It is written: 'Man shall not live on bread alone, but on every word that comes from the mouth of God'" (Mt 4:4; quoting Deut 8:3). God speaks, and his words can be our food for life. Daoism, for all its allures, dares not even offer that nourishment.

six

CHRISTIANITY

"Before Abraham was born, I am."

J ews take the Bible to be what Christians call the Old Testament. A more neutral description for what Jews identify as the Bible is the Hebrew Bible. Of course, Christianity is organically associated with the Hebrew Bible, since Jesus was a Jew who affirmed the truth of the Hebrew Bible and because the New Testament claims to fulfill or complete the Hebrew Bible. Islam, as we will see, claims to fulfill both the Hebrew Bible and the New Testament; in fact, it claims to abrogate Christianity as the normative religion.

This may all seem confusing, but we can get to the bottom of it by asking a few questions. Is Christianity a fulfillment of Judaism in that the New Testament is harmoniously related to the Hebrew Bible? Can Islam and its Qur'an rightly be considered the ultimate revelation of God, which usurps the authority of both Judaism and Christianity? In this chapter, we address one key statement made by Jesus that anchors Christianity in Judaism. Yet that statement by Jesus also transcends Judaism by focusing on Jesus himself. That statement was made by Jesus, who said, "Before Abraham was born, I am!" (Jn 8:58).

We saw in an earlier chapter that God revealed himself to Moses in the burning bush as *I am who I am*—a self-existent, personal, and purposive being, an actor in history through Moses and his other prophets, seers, and sages. And then came Jesus.

The story of Jesus has been told countless times, but the authoritative record is found in the four Gospels: Matthew, Mark, Luke, and John. Despite the relatively small stock of primary literary sources on Jesus, he is larger than any short (or long) discussion about him. As John wrote,

> Jesus did many other things as well. If every one of them were written down, I suppose that even the whole world would not have room for the books that would be written. (Jn 21:25)

The rest of the New Testament fills in the details about Christ, his church, and the ways of the Christian. This chapter focuses on one titanic statement made by Jesus in relation to the rest of his life and teachings. But before focusing on that statement, let me set the stage with some history.

JESUS 101

Whatever you think of him, Jesus is the most influential person in human history. Until recently, time was divided between AD and BC. Christ has been written out of this by the designation BCE (Before Common Era—or BC) and CE (Common Era—or AD). Still, the implicit reference to Christ remains. Christianity has the most adherents of any world religion (2.2 billion), and the mark of Jesus can be found worldwide in literature, art, morality, and everywhere else. As the church historian and theologian Jaroslav Pelikan put it:

Jesus of Nazareth has been the dominant figure in the history of Western culture for almost twenty centuries. If it were possible, with some sort of super magnet, to pull out of that history every scrap of metal bearing at least a trace of his name, how much would be left?[1]

This is all rather odd, considering his beginnings as a peasant born in poverty in a hick town, Nazareth. He was an outsider—neither rich, nor powerful, nor part of the religious establishment. He came out of nowhere, was baptized by a strange prophet named John the Baptist, and began an improbable ministry.

Reports claim that Jesus fearlessly took on the religious establishment, even calling them hypocrites and calling down God's judgment upon them as needed (Mt 23). So compelling was God's truth to Jesus that he attacked false religion squarely:

Then Jesus said to the crowds and to his disciples: "The teachers of the law and the Pharisees sit in Moses' seat. So you must be careful to do everything they tell you. But do not do what they do, for they do not practice what they preach. (Mt 23:1-3)

Then in what is perhaps the most severe insult ever uttered, Jesus said:

Woe to you, teachers of the law and Pharisees, you hypocrites! You travel over land and sea to win a single convert, and when you have succeeded, you make them twice as much a child of hell as you are. (Mt 23:15)

Yet he befriended and dined with the down-and-out (prostitutes and lepers) as well as the up-and-out (tax collectors, such as

---

[1]Jaroslav Pelikan, *Jesus Through the Centuries: His Place in the History of Culture* (New York: Harper and Row, 1985), 1.

Zacchaeus [Lk 19:1-11] and his disciple Matthew). While he could be fiery, he was tender as well:

> Come to me, all you who are weary and burdened, and I will give you rest. Take my yoke upon you and learn from me, for I am gentle and humble in heart, and you will find rest for your souls. For my yoke is easy and my burden is light. (Mt 11:28-30)

Jesus was an itinerant preacher who had nowhere to lay his head (Mt 8:20). He spoke openly with women about his ideas (so unbecoming of a real rabbi) and never patronized them, as Dorothy Sayers memorably wrote:

> Perhaps it is no wonder that women were first at the Cradle and last at the Cross. They had never known a man like this Man—there never has been such another. A prophet and teacher who never nagged them, never flattered or coaxed or patronized; who never made jokes about them, never treated them either as "the women, God help us!" or "The Ladies, God bless them!"; who rebuked without querulousness and praised without condescension; who took their questions and arguments seriously; who never mapped out their sphere for them, never urged them to be feminine or jeered at them for being female; who had no ax to grind and no uneasy male dignity to defend; who took them as he found them and was completely unself-conscious. There is no act, no sermon, no parable in the Gospel that borrows its pungency from female perversity; nobody could possibly guess from the words and deeds of Jesus that there was anything "funny" about woman's nature.[2]

---

[2]As cited in Douglas Groothuis, *Christian Apologetics: A Comprehensive Case for Biblical Faith*, 2nd ed. (Downers Grove, IL: IVP Academic, 2022), 492-93, Kindle.

Jesus never had to prove himself as a man, nor did he fear or leer after women. As Dietrich Bonhoeffer said, "Jesus only 'is there for others.' Jesus's 'being-for-others' is the experience of transcendence!"[3] He was "God with us" (Mt 1:22-23), with men and women equally and in ways that transcend everyday presence.[4]

Harry Blamires captures cleverly the lowly and improbable status of Jesus:

> He came. And he wasn't a great success in the world. He didn't have a brilliant career or climb the social ladder. He didn't acquire more and more prestige, status, and possessions. He didn't get on. He was more like you and me than like those expensively suited gentlemen in the glossy magazines who are surrounded, by sleek cars, sleeker women, and smart furniture. He came, by every act and word to show up the world's evil, yet never to pretend it was not a world fit for him, the divine, to be in, and on the bottom floor.[5]

Jesus was divine but entered our world on "the bottom floor" and stayed there until his departure. He would sink even lower by being raised up to suffer and die on a bloody Roman cross.

The kingdom of God was Jesus' incessant concern and passion. His first words of public ministry were, "Repent, for the kingdom of heaven has come near" (Mt 4:17). The "first word" of the gospel is repentance. God is a cosmic King who breaks into his fallen creation and human history to establish his rule and set matters right over time, sometimes quite dramatically, as with

[3]Dietrich Bonhoeffer, *Letters and Papers from Prison*, Dietrich Bonhoeffer Works 8 (Minneapolis: Fortress, 2009), 485, Kindle.

[4]See Douglas Groothuis, "Jesus' View of Women," in *On Jesus* (Belmont, CA: Wadsworth, 2003).

[5]Harry Blamires, *The Christian Mind: How Should a Christian Think?* (Vancouver, BC: Regent College, 2005), Kindle.

Jesus. For Jesus, God is decisively involved in both human and cosmic affairs. The kingdom of God is both a present and a future reality. As John Stott put it,

> For the Kingdom of God is God's dynamic rule, breaking into human history through Jesus, confronting, combating, and overcoming evil, spreading the wholeness of personal and communal wellbeing, taking possession of his people in total blessing and total demand.[6]

After casting out a demon, Jesus proclaimed, "But if it is by the Spirit of God that I drive out demons, then the kingdom of God has come upon you" (Mt 12:28).

Miracles were a regular part of Jesus' ministry, along with teaching and preaching—all of which combined to give him messianic credentials. When followers of John the Baptist questioned Jesus about his identity, he cited his matchless credentials, which fulfilled several messianic expectations:

> When John, who was in prison, heard about the deeds of the Messiah, he sent his disciples to ask him, "Are you the one who is to come, or should we expect someone else?"
>
> Jesus replied, "Go back and report to John what you hear and see: The blind receive sight, the lame walk, those who have leprosy are cleansed, the deaf hear, the dead are raised, and the good news is proclaimed to the poor. Blessed is anyone who does not stumble on account of me." (Mt 11:2-6)[7]

Jesus summarizes his words and deeds as evidence for his messianic status, which is coupled with a new manifestation of

---

[6]Douglas Groothuis, *Confronting the New Age: How to Resist a Growing Religious Movement* (Downers Grove, IL: InterVarsity Press, 1988), 52, Kindle.

[7]For how these words and deeds fulfill messianic expectations from the Hebrew Bible, see Isaiah 26:19; 29:18-19; 35:4-6; 61:1.

God's kingdom in Jesus himself, as an often misinterpreted saying of Jesus discloses:

> Once, on being asked by the Pharisees when the kingdom of God would come, Jesus replied, "The coming of the kingdom of God is not something that can be observed, nor will people say, 'Here it is,' or 'There it is,' because the kingdom of God is in your midst." (Lk 17:20-21)

Some translations have said, "The kingdom is *within you*" instead of "*in your midst*," thus giving some the license to pursue their own divine depths instead of turning to Jesus as God incarnate. Leo Tolstoy wrote a whole book on that false premise, *The Kingdom of God Is Within You*. No, the kingdom was "in their midst" because Jesus was in their midst, was with them as "God with us." He was the ultimate emissary of the kingdom and its perfect representative.

Any earnest writer must strain to give an accurate and sensible summary of Jesus Christ since he is remarkable on every level. However, we will move this chapter in the direction of Jesus' statement, *Before Abraham was born, I am* (Jn 8:58), by speaking of Jesus as a thinker and of his sense of authority.

JESUS AND THE INTELLECT

Part of establishing Jesus' credibility to make his stupendous statement is to address his worldview and ways of reasoning. Although some have disparaged Jesus as anti-intellectual, the charge does not stick. When he praised the faith of children, it concerned their wholeheartedness and innocence, not their ignorance. Several times he upbraided his disciples for not understanding his words and actions. He wanted them to be intellectually up to speed. After Philip asked Jesus to show him and the other disciples the Father, he replied, "Don't you know me, Philip, even after I have been among you such a long time? Anyone who has seen me has seen the Father. How can you say, 'Show us the Father'?" (Jn 14:9). One hears the tone of a teacher disappointed with the ineptitude of his student. Jesus was more distraught when his disciples could not properly cast out a demon, "'You unbelieving generation,' Jesus replied, 'how long shall I stay with you? How long shall I put up with you? Bring the boy to me'" (Mk 9:19). Given Jesus' presence and powers, there was no excuse to be a representative of "an unbelieving generation." On another occasion, he gave this jab: "'Are you so dull?' he asked" (Mk 7:18).

Jesus was not a raving and raging prophet who dispensed with logic in service of divine proclamations. Proclaim he did, and as a prophet (Mk 6:4). He could speak to the end of the world since he created it (Jn 1:1-3). But Jesus also reasoned with interlocuters when fruitful. Jesus displayed deft reasoning when challenged on vexing matters such as the Jews' relationship to the political authority of the Romans and on relationships in the afterlife.[8]

Disciples of the Pharisees and several Herodians asked Jesus a controversial political question. The Pharisees, powerful religious leaders of the Jews, were ardent nationalists who opposed the rule that Rome had imposed on the Jews in Palestine. The Herodians, on the other hand, were followers and defenders the Roman rulers who strictly governed Palestine. They tried to spring a trap. "Tell us then, what is your opinion? Is it right to pay the imperial tax to Caesar or not?" (Mt 22:17).

Jesus faced a dilemma. If he sided with the Pharisees, he might be seen as an insurrectionist and a dangerous element (as were the Zealots, Jews who defended violent revolution against the state). If he affirmed paying taxes, he would be viewed as capitulating to a secular and ungodly power instead of honoring God.

---

[8]See Groothuis, "Jesus' Use of Argument," in *On Jesus*.

He would be denounced as disloyal. As Matthew tells us, the Pharisees, who were no dummies, had "laid plans to trap him in his words" (Mt 22:15).

Jesus responded by asking for the coin used to pay the tax, a denarius. He asked, "Whose image is this? And whose inscription?" They replied that it was Caesar's. Jesus then said, "So give back to Caesar what is Caesar's, and to God what is God's." At this the delegation dispersed in amazement at his answer (Mt 22:18-22).

Jesus displays a cool head and sharp mind. When confronted with a classic dilemma pertaining to what we would call church-state relations, he finds a way logically to escape from between the horns of the dilemma. Jesus gives a place to the rule of Caesar under God without making Caesar God. Caesar's portrait on the coin (a bust of Tiberius) had an inscription ascribing deity to the emperor. When he differentiates Caesar from God, he strips Caesar of his supposed deity.

While not offering a developed political philosophy (no one was asking for that, anyway), Jesus shows a deep awareness of the issues involved and responds intelligently under pressure. On other occasions, Jesus shows himself to be neither a disloyal Jew nor an insurrectionist. He refers to God, not Caesar, as the "Lord of heaven and earth" (Mt 11:25) but does not abrogate temporal authority. Jesus informs Pilate, "You would have no power over me if it were not given to you from above" (Jn 19:11).[9]

Jesus believed that God had revealed truth in the Hebrew Bible and that he was teaching the truth: "If you hold to my teaching, you are really my disciples. Then you will know the truth, and the truth will set you free" (Jn 8:31-32). He often appealed to evidence and argument to back up his claims, as we

---

[9]This treatment of Matthew 22:15-23 is adapted from Groothuis, *On Jesus*, 26-27.

saw in his reply to the followers of John the Baptist. Jesus was no noncognitive mystic, and never said anything like *The Dao that can be spoken is not the eternal Dao* or that God was beyond all form, thought, or language, as does Hindu nondualism.

THE WORLDVIEW OF JESUS

In fact, Jesus evinced a coherent and confident worldview that presupposed in all his teaching and actions. He was a theist, who taught that God was a holy, personal, and relational being who was transcendent to the world but involved in it, establishing his kingdom, which would culminate at the final judgment.

> Jesus said to them, "Truly I tell you, at the renewal of all things, when the Son of Man sits on his glorious throne, you who have followed me will also sit on twelve thrones, judging the twelve tribes of Israel. (Mt 19:28)

Unlike Daoism, Buddhism, and nondualist Hinduism, the religion of Jesus is one of prayer, and the Lord's Prayer has been recited, individually and in church settings for two thousand years and around the world (Mt 6:9-13). God is "our Father in heaven," whose name (nature) must be "hallowed" or respected. Sadly, but truthfully, he taught that we fall short in this sacred obligation.

For Jesus, God is the basis of morality and the standard of all true judgments therewith. We have a duty to be virtuous before God, on account of God's nature: "Be perfect, therefore, as your heavenly Father is perfect" (Mt 5:48). Therefore, our obligation is to God first, and then to our neighbor.

> Hearing that Jesus had silenced the Sadducees, the Pharisees got together. One of them, an expert in the law, tested him with this question: "Teacher, which is the greatest commandment in the Law?"

Jesus replied: "'Love the Lord your God with all your heart and with all your soul and with all your mind.' This is the first and greatest commandment. And the second is like it: 'Love your neighbor as yourself.' All the Law and the Prophets hang on these two commandments." (Mt 22:34-40)

That is a high standard, and no one lives up to it. So, we move from Jesus' theology and morality to his account of the human condition.

When asked about divorce, Jesus answered by referring to Genesis 1–2.

"Haven't you read," he replied, "that at the beginning the Creator 'made them male and female,' and said, 'For this reason a man will leave his father and mother and be united to his wife, and the two will become one flesh'? So they are no longer two, but one flesh." (Mt 19:4-6)

Genesis tells us that humans are made in God's image and likeness, male and female. Yet something obviously went wrong. The fall occurred (Gen 3). Jesus tacitly acknowledges this when he speaks of the essential human problem as coming from the inside of a woman or a man:

"Don't you see that nothing that enters a person from the outside can defile them? For it doesn't go into their heart but into their stomach, and then out of the body." (In saying this, Jesus declared all foods clean.)

He went on: "What comes out of a person is what defiles them. For it is from within, out of a person's heart, that evil thoughts come—sexual immorality, theft, murder, adultery, greed, malice, deceit, lewdness, envy, slander, arrogance and folly. All these evils come from inside and defile a person." (Mk 7:18-23; see also Rom 3)

Jesus lists twelve items of infamy here, all of which "come from inside and defile a person." His anthropology is no less severe when he says, "If you, then, though you are evil, know how to give good gifts to your children, how much more will your Father in heaven give good gifts to those who ask him!" (Mt 7:11).

The a fortiori argument depends on the depravity of us all; and it is a sound argument.[10] What then can be done for these defiled and evil creatures? They need a rescue from God himself. Now on to our text.

BEFORE ABRAHAM WAS BORN, I AM

The setting for our text is yet another dispute between Jesus and the religious authorities. This one is heated. (I can think of no other founder of a religion who was more often in controversy over his teachings than Jesus, which speaks to his concern for truth discovered through reason.) In the midst of this dispute, Jesus authoritatively pronounces,

> You are from below; I am from above. You are of this world; I am not of this world. I told you that you would die in your sins; if you do not believe that I am he, you will indeed die in your sins. (Jn 8:23-24)

The discussion is serious, not trivial; consequential, not quotidian; it pertains to eternity, not only to time. Everything is at stake. After more contention and debate, the argument reaches a fever pitch of white-hot intensity.

> "Very truly I tell you, whoever obeys my word will never see death."

---

[10]These arguments have this logical structure: 1. The truth of P is accepted. 2. The support for the truth of Q (which is relevantly similar to P) is even stronger than that of P. 3. Therefore, if the truth of P must be accepted, then so must the truth of Q.

At this they exclaimed, "Now we know that you are demon-possessed! Abraham died and so did the prophets, yet you say that whoever obeys your word will never taste death. Are you greater than our father Abraham? He died, and so did the prophets. Who do you think you are?"

Jesus replied, "If I glorify myself, my glory means nothing. My Father, whom you claim as your God, is the one who glorifies me. Though you do not know him, I know him. If I said I did not, I would be a liar like you, but I do know him and obey his word. Your father Abraham rejoiced at the thought of seeing my day; he saw it and was glad."

"You are not yet fifty years old," they said to him, "and you have seen Abraham!"

"Very truly I tell you," Jesus answered, "before Abraham was born, I am!" At this, they picked up stones to stone him, but Jesus hid himself, slipping away from the temple grounds (John 8:51-58).

As is common in the Gospel of John, people often do not fathom what Jesus is really saying, what he means. When he claims to give eternal life, his listeners confuse this with endless life on earth as it is now. But he is speaking of the afterlife in the resurrected world (Jn 5:24-28). As he would later say at the tomb of his friend Lazarus, "I am the resurrection and the life. The one who believes in me will live, even though they die; and whoever lives by believing in me will never die" (Jn 11:25-26).

When Jesus said, "Very truly," he was using a figure of speech unique to him. It has been translated, "Verily, verily" (KJV). This means, in essence, "What I am saying is of supreme importance. Listen up!"

But what was Jesus saying? What did it mean? For one thing, what he said evoked a violent and immediate reaction. His listeners wanted to kill him then and there and end the discussion forever. This man was blaspheming God himself, wasn't he? But Jesus eluded them, since it was not yet his time to offer his life.

Jesus' use of "I am" statements in the Gospel of John sets the context for this most metaphysically potent "I am" statement. In seven statements, Jesus identifies himself with a quality he embodies and manifests. He affirms, "I am the bread of life" (Jn 6:35, 41, 48, 51); "I am the light of the world" (Jn 8:12); "I am the gate for the sheep" (Jn 10:7, 9); "I am the good shepherd" (Jn 10:11, 14); "I am the resurrection and the life" (Jn 11:25); "I am the way and the truth and the life" (Jn 14:6); "I am the true vine" (Jn 15:1, 5).

For a moment, let us return to Moses' encounter with God in the burning bush that was not consumed. God named himself "I AM WHO I AM" (Ex 3:14). Jesus' hearers knew to what he referred, and they could not countenance it. Jesus was not merely saying that he lived before Abraham. That would have been startling enough since no other human could rightly make that claim, although an angel could do so. Jesus was, rather, affirming that he existed before Abraham *as God himself.* God has existed forever, without beginning or end. Jesus, this man of controversy, was identifying as God himself, though he was a bona fide human being.

Herein is the genius, uniqueness, and scandal of Christianity. In but another controversy with the theologians of the day, Jesus said, "I and the Father are one" (Jn 10:30). This, like so many statements Jesus made, did not go over well and won him no accolades.

Again his Jewish opponents picked up stones to stone him, but Jesus said to them, "I have shown you many good works from the Father. For which of these do you stone me?"

"We are not stoning you for any good work," they replied, "but for blasphemy, because you, a mere man, claim to be God." (Jn 10:31-33)

Indeed, a mere man, a mortal, claimed to be God, the Creator of the universe. Unlike a Hindu guru, Jesus was not claiming to have discovered the divine within that is resident in all people since all is divine (pantheism). As Alan Watts wrote:

Jesus Christ knew he was God. So wake up and find out eventually who you really are. In our culture, of course, they'll say you're crazy and you're blasphemous, and they'll either put you in jail or in a nut house (which is pretty much the same thing). However if you wake up in India and tell your friends and relations, "My goodness, I've just discovered that I'm God," they'll laugh and say, "Oh, congratulations, at last you found out."[11]

For Watts, the pantheist, being divine is what we are in our innermost self, but that would have scandalized Jesus himself, given the best records of his life that we have, the four Gospels. For every other human who has ever existed, the claim to be God would be manifestly false. Some have claimed it, but all of them—such as Father Divine, Guru Maharah Ji, and Sun Myung Moon—have died and stayed dead. But what of Jesus?

Jesus claimed to have the authority to forgive sin and to be Lord of the Sabbath, both prerogatives of God alone (Mk 2). Moreover, he accepted worship on several occasions. Added to Jesus' self-understanding is the testimony of his followers, such as the apostles John (Jn 1:1-3) and Paul (Phil 2:5-11; Col 2:9), who confessed his deity. The creeds and confessions of the church

---

[11]Alan Watts, *Beyond Theology: The Art of Godmanship* (Novato, CA: New World Library, 2022).

have all affirmed it as well. The Apostles' Creed affirms the deity
of Christ along with that of the Father Almighty:

> I believe in God, the Father almighty,
>   creator of heaven and earth.
> I believe in Jesus Christ, his only Son, our Lord,
> who was conceived by the Holy Spirit
> and born of the virgin Mary.
> He suffered under Pontius Pilate,
> was crucified, died, and was buried;
> he descended to hell.
> The third day he rose again from the dead.
> He ascended to heaven
> and is seated at the right hand of God the Father almighty.
> From there he will come to judge the living and the dead.

We have but two choices about Jesus' claim to be God. He was
either right or he was wrong. We can rule out that he never
made these claims—that they are legendary—since they are
deeply rooted in the best documents we have about Jesus.
Matthew and John were written by followers of Jesus (Matthew
and John). Luke did careful research (Lk 1:1-4) and was a com-
panion of the apostle Paul. Scholars believe, and church history
attests, that Mark was written by a man who was guided by the
apostle Peter. We can likewise exclude the idea that Jesus did not
claim to be divine, given a straightforward reading of the passages I cited (and many others).[12]

If Jesus was wrong in claiming to be God, then he was either a
moral failure or a mental failure. Jesus would be a moral failure if
he knew he was not divine but said he was. He would then be a
liar. However, people do not lie for no reason, especially about

---

[12]See Millard J. Erickson, *The Word Became Flesh: A Contemporary Incarnational Chris-
tology* (Grand Rapids, MI: Baker Books, 1991).

matters of consequence. Given that Jesus lived in a radically monotheistic culture (and not in Alan Watts's dreamland), there would be no reason for Jesus to claim to be the God of the Old Testament if he knew he was not. That could get you killed, in fact.

The claim that Jesus was a mental failure—that he suffered from some mental illness—needs a little more work to refute, but not much more. Early in his ministry, Jesus' family thought he was out of his mind, apparently because of all the attention he was stirring up (Mk 3:20-22). However, this was only one episode, and the family is not recorded as saying it again. Others said he was possessed by demons and was casting out demons by the power of demons, a claim he refuted with simple logic (Mt 12:24-29). Jesus employs another reductio ad absurdum when the Pharisees attempt to discredit his reputation as an exorcist by charging him with driving out demons by the agency of Beelzebub, the prince of demons. In other words, they claim his reputation as a holy wonderworker is undeserved. What seem to be godly miracles really issue from a demonic being. In response, Jesus takes their premise and derives an absurdity:

> "Every kingdom divided against itself will be ruined, and every city or household divided against itself will not stand. If Satan drives out Satan, he is divided against himself. How then can his kingdom stand? And if I drive out demons by Beelzebub, by whom do your people drive them out?" (Mt 12:25-27)

Put formally:

1. If Satan were divided against himself, his kingdom would be ruined.
2. But it is not ruined (since demonic activity continues). To think otherwise is absurd.
3. Therefore (a), Satan does not drive out Satan.

4. Therefore (b), Jesus cannot free people from Satan by satanic power.

Moreover, since the Pharisees also practiced exorcism, if Jesus casts out demons by Satan, then the Pharisees must grant that they too drive out demons by Satan (Mt 12:27). But they themselves must reject this accusation as absurd. Therefore, Jesus cannot be accused of exercising satanic power through his exorcisms. He thus marshals two powerful reductio arguments in just a few sentences.[13] Even more, Jesus' rationality, compassion, and confident viewpoints do not evince the behavior of the demonic but rather the behavior of the divine.

The logic tells us that if Jesus was neither a moral failure (a liar) nor a mental failure (mentally ill), then the remaining option is that he was who he said he was—God incarnate. The logic is inescapable, unless one objection defeats the argument.

AND COULD IT BE?

When I was on a national radio program some years ago, a caller said he could not believe that Jesus was God because it was logically impossible for anyone to be God and man since deity and humanity are opposites. To be divine is to be eternal. To be human is to have a beginning. To be divine is to be omnipotent, omniscient, and omnipresent. To be human is to be finite and to possess all these attributes. Hence, the incarnation is as impossible as a triangle that has four sides! While not many voice this objection, it is worth a response, albeit brief.[14]

First, the doctrine of the incarnation must be stated correctly. Neither the Bible nor any Christian creed or confession claims

---

[13]This section is taken from Groothuis, *On Jesus*, 34-35. Portions of this section are also drawn from Douglas Groothuis, "Jesus: Philosopher and Apologist," in *Christian Research Journal*, volume 25, number 2 (2002): 28-31, 47-52.

[14]For a more developed response, see Groothuis, *Christian Apologetics*, 559-66.

that Jesus was only divine and only human since that would be a contradiction and, therefore, impossible. Rather, Jesus is one person with two natures, divine and human. That is, he is truly divine and truly human. This is analogous to—but not identical to—a person having a soul and a body but remaining one person.

But how could deity and humanity be found in the same person? The answer lies in Jesus humbling himself in leaving heaven to descend to earth for our redemption. As Paul writes of Jesus:

> Who, being in very nature God,
>> did not consider equality with God something to be
>>> used to his own advantage;
>> rather, he made himself nothing
>>> by taking the very nature of a servant,
>>> being made in human likeness.
> And being found in appearance as a man,
>> he humbled himself
>> by becoming obedient to death—
>>> even death on a cross! (Phil 2:6-8)

While Jesus did not cease to be divine, he did voluntarily suspend the use of some of his divine prerogatives and powers. We can liken this to a great baseball pitcher, such as Hall of Famer Bob Gibson (1935–2020) in his prime, playing a pickup game with some teenagers. Gibson would reserve his pitching excellence in order not to overwhelm the boys he is playing with. Nevertheless, he did not lack pitching prowess.

Philosophers and theologians have explored what is called "the logical coherence of the incarnation" in great detail, but I hope I have indicated that the doctrine is not contradictory, even if it is a bit mysterious and wonderful.[15]

---

[15]Logically, all that is needed to refute a claim that some idea P is contradictory is to give a credible way to construe the idea P that is not contradictory. While this cannot be done for the idea of a triangle with four sides, it can be done for the incarnation.

I AM IS EVERYTHING

That a Jewish peasant in ancient Palestine declared himself God is not some religious oddity, nor is it unrelated to the whole system of Christian doctrine. It is, rather, integral to the entire biblical account of reality. Of course, I cannot begin to make that case, but I can illustrate it with one statement from Paul:

> The Son is the image of the invisible God, the firstborn over all creation. For in him all things were created: things in heaven and on earth, visible and invisible, whether thrones or powers or rulers or authorities; all things have been created through him and for him. He is before all things, and in him all things hold together. And he is the head of the body, the church; he is the beginning and the firstborn from among the dead, so that in everything he might have the supremacy. For God was pleased to have all his fullness dwell in him, and through him to reconcile to himself all things, whether things on earth or things in heaven, by making peace through his blood, shed on the cross. (Col 1:15-20)

Christ made God visible, as his "image" (see also Jn 1:18). Some have taken firstborn to mean that Jesus is a created being, even the greatest created being, but the term can also mean the one who has preeminence or "supremacy," which is the meaning here in context. He cannot be created since "in him all things were created" and "he is before all things" (see also Jn 1:1-3). Even more, "in him all things hold together," which means he continues to support and uphold the created order (divine conservation). Thus, creation is rooted in the one who became incarnate. Creation and redemption are from one divine agent. It was fitting for Christ to incarnate the divine fullness, given that he created the natural world as well as the spiritual world. Christ is the head not only of creation but of the church since he redeemed it by making "peace through his blood" (his death on the cross) and because he is "the firstborn from among the dead (his resurrection). His suffering and death was an offering to God to atone for our sin against a holy God. Jesus referred to his death as liberating for humanity. He affirmed that "the Son of Man did not come to be served, but to serve, and to give his life as a ransom for many" (Mt 20:28). His death by Roman execution was not a failure, but ultimately the purpose of his coming: "The reason my Father loves me is that I lay down my life—only to take it up again. No one takes it from me, but I lay it down of my own accord. I have authority to lay it down and authority to take it up again. This command I received from my Father" (Jn 10:17-18).[16]

In my brief exposition, we find that the deity of Christ is intrinsically and integrally related to creation, conservation, redemption, and the church. Without the divine Christ, neither creation nor redemption has any purchase on reality. Pascal writes in the spirit of Paul's passage:

> Not only do we only know God through Jesus Christ, but we only know ourselves through Jesus Christ; we only know life and death through Jesus Christ. Apart from Jesus Christ we cannot know the meaning of our life or our death, of God or of ourselves. Thus without Scripture, whose only object is Christ, we know nothing and can see nothing but obscurity and confusion in the nature of God and in nature itself.[17]

WE ARE BECAUSE OF I AM

The biblical claim is nothing less than that we exist because Christ, as Creator, is the great "I am." We continue to exist because we

---

[16]On the significance of the atoning work of Christ, see Groothuis, *Christian Apologetics*, 511-48, Kindle.

[17]Blaise Pascal, *Pensées*, trans. A. J. Krailsheimer (New York: Penguin, 1966), (417/548).

are in Christ's cosmic grip. Our redemption is made possible because the "I am" lived among us, died, rose again, and ascended back to his place in the heavenly Trinity, where he now reigns before his glorious return, which is the "blessed hope" of the church (Titus 2:12-13).

Where does Christ stand in light of our other sentences? When Jesus said, *Before Abraham was born, I am*, he marked himself off from all religious founders and all people. He was claiming to be identical to the God who told Moses that his name was, "I am who I am" (Ex 3:14). He alone was the fulfillment of the Jewish prophets, who yearned for Messiah to come. He was the true man, whose obedience to truth substituted for our failure to obey. He was the true sacrifice for sin, anticipated in the Jewish law.

Jesus did not abandon logic and language to an unknowable Dao or ineffable Brahman. He brought God and truth to earth for us all to know. Jesus could not say, "Thou are that" (second person) because he alone was God in the flesh (first person). He was not simply a sage who discovered enlightenment; he was the light of the world (Jn 8:12). He was a prophet of God, but more than a prophet since he was God himself. So, in this one sentence, we see a concise yet complex philosophical and theological statement that both fulfills Jewish expectations and sets the way of Jesus apart from all other faiths. He was—and is—"I am."

- seven -

ISLAM

"There is one God, and Muhammad is his prophet."

The creed of Islam is simple, direct, and forceful: *There is one God, and Muhammad is his prophet.* It is called the *Shahadah.* This creed has been promoted and affirmed around the world since the seventh century. Islam has not shied from coercion for conversion and subjection, as we will see. Religious scholar Stephen Prothero's book *God Is Not One* orders chapters according to the degree of influence religion had in the world when he wrote in 2010. Islam is placed first.[1] He placed Christianity second, although its total adherents outnumber Islam. There are approximately 1.5 billion Muslims in the world and approximately 3.85 million in America as of 2020.[2]

---

[1]Stephen Prothero, *God Is Not One: The Eight Rival Religions That Rule the World* (New York: HarperOne, 2011).

[2]Besheer Mohamed, "Muslims Are a Growing Presence in US," Pew Research Center, September 1, 2021, www.pewresearch.org/fact-tank/2021/09/01/muslims-are-a-growing -presence-in-u-s-but-still-face-negative-views-from-the-public/.

One God, One Book

Muhammad was born in a religiously pluralistic Mecca, Arabia, in AD 570. Surrounded by various deities, a vague monotheism that acknowledged Allah (the Arabic word for "the God"), Judaism, and heretical forms of Christianity, Muhammad sought something better, and he often retreated to a cave outside of Mecca to pray and meditate. Over several retreats, starting in AD 610, he reportedly heard the voice of the angel Gabriel speak to him, saying, "Recite." He listened, recited, but did not transcribe, since he was said to be illiterate. This was the beginning of the 114 *surahs* (or chapters) of the Qur'an (or Koran) received from Allah through the angel.

Muhammad later recited these *surahs* for his followers, who would write them down on anything handy. Eventually these texts were collected into one volume, which became the sacred Scripture of Islam. The Qur'an is usually interpreted through later documents known as the Hadith, or sayings or accounts of the life of Muhammad. These are rated as to their credibility. Before looking at Muhammad and the Shahadah more closely, we can summarize Islam's six core tenets and five pillars.

Islam 101: Six Tenets, Five Pillars

Islam is emphatically monotheistic, claiming that God has no partner. It thus denies the Trinity, the incarnation, and the belief that humans are made in God's image (which would place them too close to Allah). This God alone must be worshiped and obeyed. The Qur'an and the example of Muhammad guide Islam as sources of sacred knowledge. Monotheism is the first of six tenets of Islam.

The second tenet is the existence of spirits, either good or evil. The good spirits (or angels) do the will of Allah. Gabriel is credited as revealing the Qur'an to Muhammad. Evil spirts, led by Satan, opposed the will of Allah.

Third, Allah speaks to humanity through prophets. Islam recognizes the prophets of the Hebrew Bible (while denying many of their teachings, especially those related to Jesus' deity and atonement), and it considers Jesus to be a prophet with a special standing as sinless and as a miracle worker who taught the straight path of Allah. However, it was not fitting for a prophet to die a horrible death by crucifixion so God saved him from that and delivered him to heaven, whence he will one day return. Muhammad is deemed the last and greatest prophet, "the seal of the prophets." The book of prophesy is closed with the stamp of Muhammad, and the Qur'an gives the definitive interpretation of all previous prophets.

The fourth tenet is that some of the prophets of Allah wrote holy books. Moses gave the Torah (*Taurat*), David gave the Psalms (*Zabur*), and Jesus gave the Gospel *(Injil).* In a sense, this authenticates the Bible, but not entirely. Big chunks of Scripture, such as the Prophets and Wisdom literature, are not directly included. Moreover, according to Christianity, Jesus did not write a Gospel but taught it and lived it. His story is written by the four canonical Gospel writers.

Tenet five affirms that there will be a Last Judgment by Allah. One will either end up in paradise or in hell based on one's good works and the mercy of Allah (Q Yā Sīn 36:54; Q al-Najm 53:38). The Muslim hopes that his or her good deeds will outweigh the bad deeds, but even this does not assure the Muslim of paradise; it simply gives one a better chance. The only assurance of gaining paradise is to die in an authorized jihad. If so, one goes directly to paradise. Notably, the Qur'an threatens eternal punishment in nearly every one of its 114 chapters.

The sixth tenet of Islam is that Allah predestines all that occurs. He is sovereign and his will cannot be thwarted (Q al-Qamar 54:49). While Christians disagree on the nature and meaning of God's sovereignty, Islam affirms a divine determinism that would make a hyper-Calvinist blush.[3] Nevertheless, the Qur'an also speaks of human responsibility before Allah.[4]

Alongside these six tenets are the five pillars of Muslim obedience or religious practice, the first of which is our sentence—the confession, offered sincerely, of one God and one final prophet, Muhammad. No initiation rite is added to this verbal affirmation, and Islam does not teach that something changes within the person who submits to Allah and confesses allegiance. In fact, "Islam" means submission. This differs from the biblical claim that one who confesses Christ as Lord is born again and becomes a new creature, set right with God forever (Jn 1:12-13; 3:1-21; 2 Cor 5:17).

Second, the Muslim must pray five times in a prescribed manner involving ritual cleansing, facing Mecca. This is the *Salat*. The Denver International Airport contains two small chapels, one for Muslims and one for non-Muslims. This is significant for two reasons. First, non-Muslims are not allowed to set foot in or bow the knee in a Muslim place of worship. It is not welcome to all. Second, given their public and prescribed manner of worship five times a day, when the Muslim presence increases in a country, so too does the need for public recognition of Islam.

---

[3]On God's sovereignty from a Christian perspective, see the classic statement from the Westminster *Confession of Faith* (1646), chap. 3, "Of God's Eternal Degree," www.pcaac .org/wp-content/uploads/2022/04/WCFScripureProofs2022.pdf.

[4]I will not try to resolve this or compare it to Calvinism, since that is not the burden of this chapter. See Sam Shamoun, "Qur'an Contradiction: The Problem of Divine Sovereignty, Predestination, Salvation and Human Free Will," *Answering Islam: A Christian-Muslim Dialog* (blog), accessed January 5, 2023, www.answering-islam.org/Quran /Contra/predestination.html.

Third, Muslims are required to give 2.5 percent of their profits to an Islamic charity. This is the *Zakat* and is far less than the commonly accepted minimum of 10 percent giving affirmed by Christians, and a concept rooted in the Old Testament.

Fourth, one of the most strenuous activities of Muslim spirituality is the annual observance of Ramadan, a month-long fast during daylight. Muslims can eat during the rest of the day. This is meant to quicken Muslim devotion and to acknowledge the poor.

Fifth, every Muslim is obligated to make a pilgrimage to Mecca (*Hajj*) at least once in their lifetime if possible. If they cannot, they can sponsor a surrogate. Mecca is the most religiously nondiverse place on earth since only Muslims are allowed to be there. While there, Muslims dress in white and perform various rituals.

MEET MUHAMMAD

Muhammad began his work by claiming to be a prophet to the Jews and Christians of Mecca. He failed to convince them of his prophetic mantle and was driven out and fled to Medina (the Hegira, or flight). The erstwhile prophet had far more success there, where he became a religious, political, and military leader in short order. He returned to Mecca with soldiers, destroyed the 365 idols on the sacred rock (the Kaaba), and installed himself as supreme leader. From here, he began his reign and conquest of as much of the known world as he was able.

By his death in AD 632, Muhammad was the religious and political leader of much of the Arabian Peninsula. While tracing the exploits of Muhammad—a man considered the model human for 1.5 billion people worldwide—is fascinating and controversial, it behooves us simply to ask the question, "Was Muhammad a Prophet?" since this is the second affirmation of the *Shahadah* and is inextricably related to the first: "There is one God."

Muhammad was a reformer like no other, given this reorganization of religion, politics, and society in general within his lifetime. His posthumous influence rivals that of Jesus. Whether he was a prophet from God, of course, is another question. We can first treat Muhammad's view of God and then further question his claim to prophethood.

THE ONENESS OF GOD

We must consider two aspects of Muhammad regarding his view of God as one. First, he claims to agree with the prophets of the Hebrew Bible and with Jesus himself. Second, he denies essential claims made by Hebrew prophets and by Jesus himself. Let us establish the incompatibility with his teaching on God with that of the Bible, then look at the trustworthiness of the biblical testimony.

The Qur'an says much about Jesus, claiming that he was born of a virgin (Q Maryam 19:20), was sinless, worked miracles, and was a prophet of Allah (Q al-Baqarah 2:136). It even calls him "the Messiah" (Q al-Nisā' 4:157). However, it denies his deity and his death on the cross (Q al-Nisā' 4:157). My chapter on Christianity argued that Jesus claimed to be God on earth, the great "I am" (Jn 8:58). Muhammad denies this since Allah has no son. To claim that would be the unforgiveable sin of *shirk*, or aligning anything with the utterly transcendent Allah (Q al-Mā'idah 5:17). The Qur'an identifies the idea of "the Son of God" as Allah begetting another being, his son. This is not what the Bible teaches, since the Son is eternally the Second Person of the Trinity.

In the beginning was the Word, and the Word was with God, and the Word was God. He was with God in the beginning. Through him all things were made; without him nothing was made that has been made. (Jn 1:1-3)

Muhammad also explicitly denied the Trinity, although he did not understand its meaning, thinking, the Trinity was made up of God, Jesus (who was created by God), and Mary (Q al-Nisā' 4:171). According to the New Testament, the Father, eternal Son, and Holy Spirit are equally divine but different persons. They are coequal, coeternal, and in the deepest harmony on all matters. For example, the Father, Jesus, and the Holy Spirit are all mentioned at Jesus' baptism (Mt 3), and Jesus commands his disciples to baptize converts "in the name of the Father and of the Son and of the Holy Spirit" (Mt 28:19). Of course, one could go on about the Trinity, which is the key doctrine that differentiates and distinguishes Christianity from any other monotheistic religion. The historic Anglican statement of faith, the *Thirty-nine Articles*, captures it well:

> There is but one living and true God, everlasting, without body, parts or passions; of infinite power, wisdom and goodness; the Maker, and Preserver of all things both visible and invisible. And in unity of this Godhead there be three Persons, of one substance, power, and eternity; the Father, the Son, and the Holy Ghost.

Because Muhammad denied the Trinity, he likewise denied the possibility of affirming that "God is love" (1 Jn 4:8). While Allah is called "merciful," his mercy does not flow from his inner being as love. Love requires a lover, a loving, and a beloved. The Bible teaches that before the creation, God lived eternally in a loving relationship with himself as Father, Son, and Holy Spirit. As C. S. Lewis wrote:

> Being Christians, we learn from the doctrine of the Blessed Trinity that something analogous to "society" exists within the Divine being from all eternity—that God is Love, not

merely in the sense of being the Platonic form of love, but because, within Him, the concrete reciprocities of love exist before all worlds and are thence derived to the creatures.[5]

Allah, being absolutely unitary, requires creatures in order to be loving. The Trinity is love eternal and shows love through the incarnation of Christ.[6]

The Hebrew Prophets and Muhammad

But what of the Hebrew Bible and its prophets? Muhammad claims he is a prophet as well as they are; they are prophets of the one true God if prophets all must agree as to the nature and purposes of the God for whom they speak. Consider a sampling of prophetic statements from the Hebrew Bible.

Isaiah writes of the coming Messiah:

For to us a child is born,
   to us a son is given,
   and the government will be on his shoulders.
And he will be called
   Wonderful Counselor, Mighty God,
   Everlasting Father, Prince of Peace.
Of the greatness of his government and peace
   there will be no end.
He will reign on David's throne
and over his kingdom,
   establishing and upholding it
   with justice and righteousness
   from that time on and forever.

---

[5]C. S. Lewis, *The Problem of Pain*, Collected Letters of C. S. Lewis (New York: Harper-Collins, 2001), 21, Kindle.

[6]For more on this, see Jonah Haddad and Douglas Groothuis, "Allah, the Trinity, and Divine Love," *Christian Research Journal* 36, no. 5 (2013), www.equip.org/PDF/JAF5365 .pdf.

The zeal of the Lord Almighty
   will accomplish this. (Is 9:6-7)[7]

The coming one is divine, and his governance will have no end. Surely, a man claiming the prophet's mantle would not usurp or contradict his divine rule. But that is what Muhammad has done. Listen to Isaiah again, speaking of the coming suffering servant.

Who has believed our message
   and to whom has the arm of the Lord been revealed?
He grew up before him like a tender shoot,
   and like a root out of dry ground.
He had no beauty or majesty to attract us to him,
   nothing in his appearance that we should desire him.
He was despised and rejected by mankind,
   a man of suffering, and familiar with pain.
Like one from whom people hide their faces
   he was despised, and we held him in low esteem.

Surely he took up our pain
   and bore our suffering,
yet we considered him punished by God,
   stricken by him, and afflicted.
But he was pierced for our transgressions,
   he was crushed for our iniquities;
the punishment that brought us peace was on him,
   and by his wounds we are healed.
We all, like sheep, have gone astray,
   each of us has turned to our own way;

---

[7]For a detailed case that these verses refer to Jesus Christ, see Michael L. Brown, *Answering Jewish Objections to Jesus*, 2 vols. (Grand Rapids, MI: Baker Books, 2000); and Walter C. Kaiser Jr., *The Messiah in the Old Testament*, rev. ed. (Grand Rapids, MI: Zondervan, 1995).

and the LORD has laid on him
    the iniquity of us all. (Is 53:1-6)

Many more texts could be cited, but the Hebrew prophets speak with one voice of one Messiah, Jesus Christ, who provides atonement for sin, something denied by Muhammad.[8]

MUHAMMAD AND THE ATONEMENT

Muhammad and all of Islam since its inception deny that Jesus suffered and died to atone for our sins against God. Islam is concerned about sin, to be sure, but it prescribes good deeds as the antidote to sin in the hopes that one's good deeds will outweigh the bad and paradise be one's fate. Allah is known as "most merciful," but his mercy is not guaranteed, even for the most observant Muslim. Near the end of Ramadan, Muslims fervently pray that Allah will forgive their sins since the tradition claims that on "the night of power," which commemorates Muhammad's receiving the Qur'an, their prayers are more powerful than on other days.

By comparison, given the testimony about Jesus, his followers are assured that their sins are forgiven upon their confession of faith. Many passages illustrate this, but here is just one.

Yet to all who did receive him, to those who believed in his name, he gave the right to become children of God— children born not of natural descent, nor of human decision or a husband's will, but born of God. (Jn 1:12-13; see also Jn 3:1-8)

While Muhammad claimed to be a prophet in the inspired lineage of the Hebrew prophets and Jesus, his claims ring unconvincing in light of Jesus' teaching about himself. The Bible

---

[8]Kaiser, *Messiah in the Old Testament.*

agrees with the Qur'an that Jesus was a prophet, sinless, born of a virgin, and a worker of miracles and that he ascended into heaven. But Jesus himself contradicts the Qur'an about his own identity. For example, in Mark, Jesus makes at least two claims to his own deity. He claimed he had the authority to forgive sins, which is a uniquely divine prerogative (Mk 2:1-12). He further claimed that "the Son of Man is Lord even of the Sabbath" (Mk 2:23-28), another claim of divine authority since God created and ordained the Sabbath (Gen 2:1-3).

One of the most direct claims to deity made by Jesus is the subject of our chapter on Christianity, but I advert to it briefly. At the end of a dispute about Jesus' identity, we read: "'Very truly I tell you,' Jesus answered, 'before Abraham was born, I am!' At this, they picked up stones to stone him" (Jn 8:58-59). By "I am," Jesus meant the name God used for himself when he talked to Moses (Ex 3:13-16). His interlocuters realized this so they tried to stone him for blasphemy. But Jesus' death would require crucifixion, not stoning, since it had been foretold (Is 53:1-6).

Jesus, a human being, even accepted the worship of his disciples, something unheard of in Islam and considered blasphemous. After Jesus walked on water, "those who were in the boat worshiped him, saying, 'Truly you are the Son of God'" (Mt 14:33). After his resurrection, Jesus received worship from several women (Mt 28:8-9) as well as from his disciple, Thomas (Jn 20:28). Jesus never corrected those who worshiped him, as we find happening with other biblical characters (Acts 10:25-26; Rev 19:9-10). As a Jew, Jesus knew that God alone should be worshiped, as seen when Jesus refused to worship the devil (Lk 4:5-8).

Besides Jesus himself, the apostle John affirmed the deity of Jesus in John 1:1-3 (and elsewhere), as quoted earlier, as did Paul:

In your relationships with one another, have the same mindset as Christ Jesus:

Who, being in very nature God,
    did not consider equality with God something to be
        used to his own advantage;
rather, he made himself nothing
    by taking the very nature of a servant,
    being made in human likeness. (Phil 2:5-7)

And again, "For in Christ all the fullness of the Deity lives in bodily form" (Col 2:9). Speaking of "the people of Israel," Paul writes: "Theirs are the patriarchs, and from them is traced the human ancestry of the Messiah, who is God over all, forever praised! Amen" (Rom 9:4-5).

Both the Hebrew Bible and the New Testament contradict Muhammad's claims about God and Jesus Christ. The Bible and the Qur'an cannot both be correct. To be credible, Muhammad or the Qur'an would have to offer a compelling reason to override the judgments of the Bible about these crucial doctrines. That is an uphill battle since the Qur'an appeals to no new historical evidence to discredit the Bible on these matters. Rather, a religious seeker went into a cave and heard a voice. The Qur'an itself endorses the divine authority of the Bible (Q al-Nisā' 4:48, 136; Q al-Mā'idah 5:47-51, 68-71; Q Yūnus 10:94). The Qur'an also tells the reader to consult the Christian Scriptures to corroborate the veracity of Muhammad's message and his status as a prophet:

But if you are in doubt as to what We have revealed to you, ask those who read the Book before you; certainly the truth has come to you from your Lord, therefore you should not be of the disputers (Q Yūnus 10:94; see also Q al-Mā'idah 5:47-51, 72; Q Maryam 19:29-30; Q al-Anbiyā' 21:7; Q al-'Ankabūt 29:46-47).

Thus, the Qur'an endorses the divine inspiration of Scripture, and it holds that those Scriptures endorse Muhammad. This raises an insuperable problem for Islam, however, since the copies of both testaments during the time of Muhammad were substantially the same as what we have today, even though Islam claims the Bible had been corrupted. As Old Testament scholar Gleason Archer notes:

> It is completely out of the question to discredit the text of Holy Scripture as no longer conforming to what was current in Muhammad's time, from A.D. 610-632. Complete manuscripts of the New Testament copied out in the fourth century (Codex Vaticanus and Codex Sinaiticus) and the fifth century (Codex Alexandrinus), antedate the revelation of the Qur'an by three centuries.[9]

Therefore, when the Qur'an says to consult the Christian Scriptures for the verification of the truth of Islam, it contradicts itself since, as we have shown, the extant Christian Scriptures of Muhammad's day teach that God is a Trinity, that Christ is the incarnation of God, and that salvation is through faith in Jesus Christ—all doctrines that Islam rejects.

Another striking fact about Muhammad's supposed prophethood is that he is neither predicted in the Bible (as is Jesus) nor does he make any predictions that have been fulfilled (unlike Jesus). Muslims claim that Muhammad is the prophet predicted in Deuteronomy 18, but that is refuted because the coming prophet will be Jewish, not Arabian, as was Muhammad. This prophecy was fulfilled by Jesus.[10]

---

[9]Gleason Archer, "Confronting the Challenge of Islam in the 21st Century," in *Contend for the Faith: Collected Papers of the Rockford Conference on Discernment and Evangelism*, ed. Eric Pement (Chicago: Evangelical Ministries to New Religions, 1992), 96.
[10]Nabeel Qureshi, *Seeking Allah, Finding Jesus*, 3rd ed. (Grand Rapids, MI: Zondervan, 2018), 252-53.

Muslims further claim that Jesus predicted the coming of Muhammad in his references to the *paraclete,* which can be translated as "Helper" (ESV), "Comforter" (KJV), or "Advocate" (NIV). In John's Gospel, Jesus said he would ask the Father to give his disciples "another advocate to help you and be with you forever—the Spirit of truth." (Jn 14:16-17). He then identifies the Advocate as the Holy Spirit, who will be sent "in my name, will teach you all things and will remind you of everything I have said to you" (Jn 14:26). Jesus reaffirms what he said earlier by saying "When the Advocate comes, whom I will send to you from the Father—the Spirit of truth who goes out from the Father—he will testify about me" (Jn 15:26). Last, Jesus promises that when he goes away, he will send "the Advocate" (Jn 16:7). Putting these together, we find that the Advocate will be with his disciples forever. Muhammad died in the seventh century. Moreover, Muhammad did not speak the truth about Jesus, as we have seen. He is no Holy Spirit, whom the Bible says is divine (Acts 5:3-4; 2 Cor 13:14).[11]

Muhammad's status as a prophet is overturned by these evidential observations. Moreover, while no biblical prophet was morally perfect (spare Jesus), they were men and women of good moral standing. The same cannot be said of Muhammad, given his marriage to a six-year-old girl (Ayasha), his treachery in warfare, his vengeful actions, his violence against Jews and Christians, and much more.[12] Both Mark Gabriel, who taught Islamic history at Al-Azar University in Cairo, Egypt, and Nabeel Qureshi, a devout young American Muslim, rejected Islam for these (and other) reasons and became Christians and have defended Christianity against Islam.[13]

---

[11]See also Qureshi, *Seeking Allah,* 253-54.
[12]See Robert Spencer, *The Truth About Muhammad* (Washington, DC: Regnery, 2006).
[13]See Mark A. Gabriel, *Jesus and Muhammad* (Lake Mary, FL: Charisma House, 2004); Qureshi, *Seeking Allah;* and Robert Spencer, *The Religion of Peace? Why Christianity Is and Islam Isn't* (Washington, DC: Regnery, 2007).

After teaching, studying, and writing about Islam for decades, I am convinced that Islam's effect has not been for the good of the world overall. Islam from the beginning has been territorial; it has aspired to be a civilization, not merely a religion chosen by those inclined to believe. To use Bernard Lewis's term, it has aspired to be "Islamdom," a global civilization ruled by Islamic law—a law that forbids freedom of religion and equal rights to women. Islamdom would be a theocracy in which other religions are not tolerated.[14] In an Islamic society, Jews and Christians become *dhimmis*, or "protected people." They are protected from other Muslims who would want to kill them, but their religious activities are controlled by Islamic authorities who also extract a poll tax from them. Rumors to the contrary, this is nothing like religious freedom as understood in the West generally and in America in particular.

THE BIBLE AND THE QUR'AN

The Qur'an teaches that Christians and Jews are "people of the Book." As such, they deserve a higher status in an Islamic society than polytheists or those who defect from Islam. Historically, the latter have faced the sword. However, Christians take their Bible to be far different from how Muslims view their Qur'an. The orthodox account of the Bible's inspiration is that an infinite personal being used his image-bearers to write what he deemed fit for his own glory and for the expansion of his kingdom. As the apostle Peter said:

> Above all, you must understand that no prophecy of Scripture came about by the prophet's own interpretation of things. For

---

[14]Bernard Lewis, "Mars Hill Audio Conversations with Ken Myers," vol. 19 (March 31, 2003). See also Alvin J. Schmidt, *The Great Divide: The Failure of Islam and the Triumph of the West* (Frederick, USA: Regina Orthodox Press, 2004).

prophecy never had its origin in the human will, but prophets, though human, spoke from God as they were carried along by the Holy Spirit. (2 Pet 1:20-21; see also 2 Tim 3:15-16)

The many and diverse authors of Scripture were "carried along by the Holy Spirit." They did not relinquish their personalities, nor were they abstracted from their providential place in space and time. Thus, the inspiration of the sixty-six books of the Old and New Testaments is confluent—from both God and humans. This is fitting since humans bear the image of God (Gen 1:26-27). People without divine inspiration will make errors, but not when God "carries them along by the Holy Spirit." Therefore, all the teachings of Scripture—history, poetry, eschatology, morality, the cosmos—bear the touch of humanity but not the mark of falsity.[15] The Bible, then, intersects our world at every turn since its many authors wrote at different times and places. Therefore, we find that the Bible is corroborated by archaeology and extra-biblical history. Scripture is not one burst of divine information supposedly given to one person in a short period of time.

Muslims believe that the 114 chapters (or *surahs*) of the Qur'an were given to Muhammad through the angel Gabriel from about AD 610–632. As an illiterate, Muhammad made no contribution to the divine utterances his received. Rather, he memorized and recited them. His followers inscribed these revelations over several years, and they were compiled after Muhammad's death. Variant sayings were destroyed by Uthmān ibn 'Affān (d. 656), the third caliph of Islam.

Islam teaches that the Qur'an is a wholly divine book. No human had anything to do with its authorship, and it is only

---

[15]For the treatment of difficulties with the Bible, see Gleason L. Archer Jr., *New International Encyclopedia of Biblical Difficulties* (Grand Rapids, MI: Zondervan, 2001); and Norman L. Geisler and Thomas Howe, *The Big Book of Bible Difficulties*, pbk. ed. (Grand Rapids, MI: Baker Books, 2008).

authoritative when read in its original Arabic. Renderings into other languages are not called translations but are identified as interpretations. Allah speaks ancient Arabic, the language he dictated to Gabriel, who related it to a young man meditating in a cave in AD 610.

Unlike the Bible, the Qur'an does not offer itself to history as a verifiable document, rooted in the witness of many authors over hundreds of years. What it gets right, it takes from the Bible (such as the virgin birth of Jesus); what it gets wrong is titanic: Jesus was not God, he did not die on a cross or rise again, and salvation does not come by grace through faith in Jesus Christ. And it offers no good reason to believe any of its contradictions to biblical claims.

The Bible and the Qur'an, while deemed holy by their adherents, really have little in common. The Bible's inspiration honors human authors but not at the expense of divine revelation, it is grounded in verifiable history, and it brings the good tidings of the gospel. The Qur'an, while supposedly the very words of Allah, is merely human,[16] cannot be verified by history, and brings a hopeless message of salvation by good works offered to a terribly distorted idea of God.

ONE GOD, NO PROPHET

The subtitle you just read would commit the crime of blasphemy in some Muslim countries today. For example, in Pakistan at least seventeen people "were sentenced to death on blasphemy charges in 2019, including a university lecturer accused of having insulted the Prophet Muhammad verbally and on Facebook." However, the government has not executed anyone for blaspheming Islam

---

[16]Given the claim that the Qur'an was delivered by an angel, it is possible that a fallen angel had something to do with the content of the Qur'an. On this, see Galatians 1:8-10, 2 Corinthians 11:13-14, and 1 John 4:1-3.

yet.[17] Yet in countries that establish and ensure the freedom of religion and speech, such as the United States, one is free to reach a reasoned conclusion about Islam and its purported prophet.

I am free to deny Muhammad as a prophet, and you are free to affirm Muhammad as a prophet and to deny that Jesus is God incarnate. The state will not arbitrate between our consciences, and we should all thank God for that. My conclusion is that, given the evidence, while Muhammad was right in the broad contours of his monotheism (and his opposition to polytheism), he was terribly wrong on Jesus Christ, the way of salvation, and the triune nature of God. In response to our chosen sentence, then: Yes, there is One God, but Muhammad is not his prophet since no prophet of God would deny that Jesus is the Christ in the biblical sense.

Who is the liar? It is whoever denies that Jesus is the Christ. Such a person is the antichrist—denying the Father and the Son. No one who denies the Son has the Father; whoever acknowledges the Son has the Father also.

As for you, see that what you have heard from the beginning remains in you. If it does, you also will remain in the Son and in the Father. And this is what he promised us—eternal life. (1 Jn 2:22-25)

---

[17]Virginia Villa, "Four-in-Ten Countries and Territories Worldwide Had Blasphemy Laws in 2019," Pew Research Center, January 25, 2022, www.pewresearch.org/fact-tank/2022/01/25/four-in-ten-countries-and-territories-worldwide-had-blasphemy-laws-in-2019-2.

CONCLUSION

SEVEN SENTENCES, SEVEN WORLDVIEWS, AND A LITTLE LOGIC

Our seven sentences have led us into some deep and sometimes troubled waters of metaphysics, epistemology, and morality. Rather than giving a bland summary of the beliefs of the religions addressed, I have sought to engage with them philosophically and comparatively from an explicitly Christian perspective. Of course, a member of one of the other religions covered would have written a different book. A Buddhist, for example, would compare each sentence of the other worldviews with Buddhism, and mutatis mutandis for the other religions. While my philosophical analysis has not presupposed the truth of Christianity, my comparative efforts were vis-à-vis Christianity. In so doing, I hope I have commended the Christian worldview and the Christian way of life.

An apt end to a short book is a brief summary, with a few new points added for further clarity.

1. GOD IS DEAD

The atheist Friedrich Nietzsche was inducted as a foil to all religion, given his statement that *God is dead*. If he is right, then all religion is wrong. While his main target was mono-theism, he denied the existence of any sacred realm or purpose. Thus, existence was shorn of objective meaning or value. The only meaning available was to those who somehow overcome their nature (which is impossible without God), throw off all religion, and aspire to be an overman, radical self-creators. Yet they are not truly free but are fated to be what they are, given Nietzsche's doctrine of eternal recurrence. Moreover, if every-thing lacks meaning, value, and purpose, then every human being is locked up in the same metaphysical prison, with no key available.

We found that the brilliant philologist and philosopher's cri-tique of Christianity was not so brilliant, although it is striking in its audacity, intensity, and creativity. He abhorred God more than he demonstrated his nonexistence since he took Christi-anity as antilife, ascetic, and masochistic. This was a horrible caricature, however, as I argued. Although he claimed that there was not enough evidence to support theism, Nietzsche failed to address any of the plethora of theistic proofs and simply said any God worth his salt would be more evident to more people.[1] But the knowledge of God is not that simple; one must be humbly receptive in order to respond properly to God's revelation in nature and conscience (Rom 1:18-32).

2. I Am Who I Am

Jews have always identified as a "chosen people," chosen by God himself for God's redemptive purposes. God names himself "I am who I am" in his revelation to Moses (Ex 3:14). This name

---

[1]On the case for Christianity, with a strong emphasis on natural theology, see Douglas Groothuis and Andrew I. Shepardson, *The Knowledge of God in the World and the Word: An Introduction to Classical Apologetics* (Grand Rapids, MI: Zondervan Academic, 2022).

means that God is a self-reflective, purposeful, rational, and complete being—a Being unlike any other being. "God is completely self-defining, self-originating, and self-preserving."[2]

As a personal being and rational being, God creates, speaks, enacts covenants, makes promises, and orders history to the end of creating a people who will bless the entire world. Since humans are made in the image of God, they are well suited to receive communication from God in nature, from the prophets, and in Scripture. Judaism is a religion of the Word, which highly values written communication and argumentation. This is a significant part of "the gifts of the Jews" to civilization.[3] Christians believe that God's ultimate purpose for the Jews was the coming of the Messiah, who is prophesied throughout the Hebrew Bible and is fulfilled in the coming of Jesus Christ.

3. You Are That

Hinduism is a religion of many philosophical schools and varying worldviews, although common themes are found, such as karma, the caste system, reincarnation, yoga, and *moksha* (sometimes called Nirvana). The sentence for Hinduism, *You are that*, is taken from the Upanishads and interpreted by one of the philosophical schools to mean that reality is nondual and only divine. The finite self is an illusion and is really one with the Self or Brahman, an impersonal and ineffable reality. Sankara tried to save the appearances of individuality and diversity by his two-truth theory, but we found that to be untrue because it is contradictory. The claim that the all-encompassing oneness is beyond thought and language also falters when anyone tries in vain to describe it through thought and language.

---

[2]Rev. Timothy Soots, Easter message, April 17, 2022.
[3]Thomas Cahill, *The Gifts of the Jews: How a Tribe of Desert Nomads Changed the Way Everyone Thinks and Feels* (New York: Anchor Books, 1999).

Hinduism speaks of avatars as periodic manifestations of the Absolute, but no avatar is rooted in verifiable history, as is Jesus of Nazareth (Lk 1:1-4). Moreover, avatars may not represent a personal God at all. According to the Upanishads, "The one absolute impersonal Existence, together with his inscrutable Maya, appears as the divine Lord, the personal God, endowed with manifest glories."[4] According to the Bible, the personal God incarnates as the personal divine Lord. There is nothing impersonal about it.

The Word became flesh and made his dwelling among us. We have seen his glory, the glory of the one and only Son, who came from the Father, full of grace and truth. (Jn 1:14)

Avatar and incarnation stand a million miles apart, both theologically and in historical attestation.[5]

4. Life Is Suffering

Life is suffering is the doleful confession of Buddha and Buddhists, and it is the condition from which they seek liberation. Buddhism is the great *no* to life as is. Unlike Judaism and Christianity, Buddhism grants no final hope for the universe as a whole or for individuals. The Buddha, unlike Jesus, was neither an incarnation nor a prophet but a sage. His sagacity was the dharma he taught as an enlightened being. Suffering could only be overcome—and the wheel of karma stopped—by freeing oneself from desire and in so doing eventually attaining Nirvana, a condition largely beyond description since it is pure negation.

Buddhism is an austere and ascetic worldview, but human beings seek sanctuary and comfort in life. To that end, Buddhists claim to find refuge in three things:

---

[4] *The Upanishads: Breath of the Eternal*, selected and trans. Swami Prabhavananda and Frederick Manchester (New York: Mentor Books, 1957), 121.
[5] Geoffrey Parrinder, *Avatar and Incarnation: The Divine in Human Form in the World's Religions* (Rockport, MA: Oneworld, 1997).

I take refuge in the Buddha.

I take refuge in the Dharma.

I take refuge in the Sangha. (Buddhist community)

These are known as the three jewels or the three treasures. Taking refuge in Buddha is really the same as taking refuge in the dharma since Buddha woke up and found the dharma. As a person, Buddha offers nothing but dharma and his example since he had died and attained Nirvana. He has no agency in the world of suffering. The Buddhist community is one of ritual, belief, and experience but not of worship based on God's redemption of his creatures. Later Buddhism sometimes deems Buddha a kind of savior figure to be venerated, but this does not fit well with his original and essential teachings.

Contrariwise, Christians can affirm:

I take refuge in the Christ.

I take refuge in the Gospel.

I take refuge in the church.[6]

Refuge in Christ goes beyond appreciation of this teaching or veneration for his person. Christians are "in Christ," as Paul often affirms. "Therefore, if anyone is in Christ, the new creation has come: The old has gone, the new is here!" (2 Cor 5:17). We have union with Christ because of his achievements on our behalf. Refuge also means being freed from the penalty of sin. "Therefore, there is now no condemnation for those who are in Christ Jesus" (Rom 8:1). Refuge is found in the gospel "because it is the power of God that brings salvation to everyone who believes" (Rom 1:16) and because its truth is powerful: "And you also were included in Christ when you heard the message of truth, the gospel of your salvation" (Eph 1:13). Christians take

---

[6]Stephen Neil, *The Supremacy of Jesus* (Downers Grove, IL: InterVarsity Press, 1984), 52.

refuge in the church since it is the body of Christ, a supernatural company of saints in which everyone has a role to play (1 Cor 12–14). And, as Jesus promised of the church, "the gates of Hades will not overcome it" (Mt 16:18).

5. The Dao That Can Be Spoken Is Not the Eternal Dao

Daoism has fewer adherents than the other religions addressed in this book. Nevertheless, many resonate with its counsel to transcend words through a mystical affinity with the depths of nature, the Dao. This Dao, or Way, cannot be conceptualized or systematized. It is beyond words. One cannot build a structure out of water, and the Dao is "the watercourse way," as Alan Watts put it.

Watts's collaborator on the book *Tao: The Watercourse Way*, Al Chung-liang Huang, speaks of Watts needing to give up controlling the Dao intellectually.[7] He illustrates this by recounting the reverie he and Watts shared after a seminar on Daoism at the Esalen Institute. "Alan turned to me and started to speak, ready to impress me with his usual eloquence about our successful week together." Huang then "noticed a sudden breakthrough in his expression: a look of lightness and glow appeared all around him. Alan had discovered a different way to tell me of his feelings."[8]

> Yah . . . Ha . . . Ho . . . Ha! Ho . . . La Cha Om Ha . . . Deg def te te . . . Ta De De Ta Te Ta . . . Ha Te Te Ha Hom . . . Te Te Te . . .

Huang says that they "gibbered and danced all the way up the hill. Everyone around understood what we were saying. Alan knew too that he had never—not in all his books—said it any

---

[7] Al Chung-liang Huang, foreword to *Tao: The Watercourse Way*, by Alan Watts (New York: Pantheon, 1975), viii.

[8] Huang, foreword to Watts, *Tao*, ix.

better than that."⁹ *The Dao that can be spoken is not the eternal Dao*, but the Dao that can be put in unintelligible sounds is something else, something better—at least for Alan Watts and his friend.

Unlike biblical religion, which stresses God's verbal communication and actions in history, Daoists delight in the gnomic, the esoteric, and the whimsical; their concern is nature, not history. They enjoy wordplay and paradox, not assertion and argument. Moses heard a divine voice in a burning bush and changed history. Laozi hears no voice and downplays words: "Man was not made to blow out air. He was made to sit quietly and find the truth within."¹⁰ Jesus gave many arguments but blew no air.¹¹ He declared that he himself was the truth offered to others who did not have the truth within themselves. "I am the way and the truth and the life. No one comes to the Father except through me" (Jn 14:6; see also Acts 4:12; 1 Tim 2:5).

6. Before Abraham Was Born, I Am

Jesus was a Jewish prophet with no official credentials within the religious establishment of his time. He lived in obscurity as a carpenter until his baptism by his cousin John. He then began to disturb, comfort, and perplex the masses through his teaching and his miracles. It was rightly said of him, "No one ever spoke the way this man does" (Jn 7:46). After preaching the Sermon on the Mount, "the crowds were amazed at his teaching, because he taught as one who had authority, and not as their teachers of the law" (Mt 7:28-29).

---

⁹Huang, foreword to Watts, *Tao*, ix.

¹⁰Lao Tzu, *Tao Te Ching*, trans. Jonathan Star (New York: Tarcher/Penguin, 2001), 6, Kindle.

¹¹See Douglas Groothuis, "Jesus' Use of Argument," in *On Jesus* (Belmont, CA: Wadsworth, 2003).

Yet Jesus said many things that shocked and outraged his hearers, such as the theological bombshell we addressed. "'Very truly I tell you,' Jesus answered, 'before Abraham was born, I am!'" (Jn 8:58). "Very truly" was an expression unique to Jesus as a teacher of his day. It is translated in the King James Version of the Bible as "Verily, verily." *The Message* translates it "Believe me." Or we might say, "You really need to hear this. I am not kidding around!" The words that followed shocked them since, as we discussed, Jesus was claiming to be God himself—the God that revealed himself to Moses (Ex 3:14). Thus, "at this, they picked up stones to stone him, but Jesus hid himself, slipping away from the temple grounds" (Jn 8:59). Although Jesus' words were often respected, these words nearly got him stoned for blasphemy.

This was not a one-off performance, though, since Jesus spoke of his deity on other occasions (Mk 2:1-12). His biographers confessed it as well (Jn 1:1-3) as did the apostle Paul (Col 2:9). This is a small sampling of the evidence. There are intimations of a divine Messiah to come in the Hebrew Bible as well (Is 9:6). This claim would be more than embarrassing for Moses, Buddha, or Muhammad to make. For Moses and Muhammad, it would be blasphemous. For Buddha, an atheist, it would be nonsensical. Yet, for Jesus, this statement fits his character and his mission. As John Stott summarized:

> Thus, to know him was to know God;
> to see him was to see God;
> to believe in him was to believe in God;
> to receive him was to receive God;
> to hate him was to hate God;
> to honour him was to honour God.[12]

---

[12]John Stott, *Basic Christianity* (Grand Rapids, MI: Eerdmans, 2017), 27, Kindle. See John 8:19; 14:1, 7, 9; 12:44, 45; Mark 9:37; John 5:23; 15:23.

If there were no God, these claims would be delusional. But science and philosophy give us plenty of reasons to believe in God.[13] If the concept of incarnation (the God-man) is not contradictory (as we argued), then it is possible. We, thus, need to investigate the evidence, and Jesus is by far the best candidate for being the incarnation of God since he would have no reason to claim to be divine unless he was divine. He had no occasion to lie, and he did not act like a man so out of his mind as to claim he was from out of this world when he was not. A Jewish peasant claimed to be God, and was. The world has never gotten over that. But not all have believed it.

7. There Is One God, and Muhammad Is His Prophet

Islam shares with Judaism and Christianity a confession of one God. It also, like Judaism and Christianity, claims Abraham as the father of faith. But the nature and meaning of that faith differs greatly from that of Judaism and Christianity.

Muhammad declared himself a prophet over five hundred years after the death of Jesus, an event he did not accept. Claiming to be "the seal of the prophets," Muhammad attempted to nullify the biblical record that Jesus was the divine Messiah who died and rose again. His authorization for this antihistorical claim was a purported revelation from an angel to himself while he meditated in a cave in Mecca.

In place of the gospel, Muhammad substituted Islamic law and the uncertain hope that if one obeyed this law sufficiently, Allah would be merciful to the Muslim and grant paradise after the Last Judgment. But Muhammad and all Muslims must face a grim and demanding logic to support their claims. For Islam

---

[13]See Douglas Groothuis, "The Case for Christian Theism," part 2 in *Christian Apologetics: A Comprehensive Case for Biblical Faith*, 2nd ed. (Downers Grove, IL: IVP Academic, 2022).

to have rational authority as the true religion, it must trump the case for Christianity since it contradicts key Christian doctrines, such as the saving death of Christ, his deity, the Trinity, and salvation received by faith because of the grace of God (Eph 2:8-9). While the story of Jesus is well supported by the four Gospels and the rest of the New Testament, Muhammad offers no new evidence from history or logic to refute the claim that "before Abraham was born, I am" (Jn 8:58). It *declares* Muhammad as prophet and *denies* cardinal Christian doctrines, but it *refutes* none of it.

Unlike Jesus, Muhammad was not foretold; nor did he foretell the future.[14] Unlike Jesus, Muhammad worked no miracles (at least as recorded in the Qur'an; later documents claim some miracles). Unlike Jesus, Muhammad intimidated, subjugated, or slew his enemies. Jesus died for them, saying from the cross, "Father, forgive them, for they do not know what they are doing" (Lk 23:34). Nor did Jesus authorize the sword to promote the cross but rested the fate of his message originally given to a few Jewish outcasts on teaching, preaching, praying, suffering, and serving (Mt 28:18-20). The first Christian martyr, Stephen, was stoned while engaged in apologetics, not in an armed battle. And, like Jesus, he called for his murderers to be forgiven.

> While they were stoning him, Stephen prayed, "Lord Jesus, receive my spirit." Then he fell on his knees and cried out, "Lord, do not hold this sin against them." When he had said this, he fell asleep. (Acts 7:59-60)

---

[14]Blaise Pascal develops this criticism in several parts of the *Pensées*.

SEVEN SENTENCES, ONE TRUTH, AND A LITTLE LOGIC

Perhaps this book could have been called *World Religions: An Opinionated Introduction* in the manner of D. A. Armstrong's book, *Universals: An Opinionated Introduction*.[15] It may be opinionated since it does not attempt to dispassionately present religious statements and let the reader draw his or her own conclusions. However, opinions may be well supported or ill advised, and the reader must draw his or her own conclusions about how that works out.

The only reason to take any of these sentences as worth believing is because one takes one or more of them to be true—to reflect the objective reality concerning the ultimate reality. And the truth of a statement should be judged in light of logic and evidence. I take only two of these statements to be true without qualification, as the attentive reader will note. But we can summarize the logic of our exposition. I will restate our sentences:

1. God is dead (Atheism).

2. I AM WHO I AM (Judaism).

3. You are that (Hinduism).

4. Life is suffering (Buddhism).

5. The Dao that can be spoken is not the eternal Dao (Daoism).

6. Before Abraham was born, I am (Christianity).

7. There is one God, and Muhammad is his prophet (Islam).

Let us run the logic of truth in terms of some of the logical implications.

1. If sentence (1) is true, then sentences (2)-(7) are all false since all religions would be false (despite Nietzsche's respect for Buddhism).

---

[15]D. M. Armstrong, *Universals: An Opinionated Introduction* (Malden, MA: Routledge, 1989).

2. If sentence (2) is true, then, sentence (6) is true (if Jesus is divine, something Jews reject), and the first half of sentence (7), *There is one God*, is true. The rest are false.

3. If sentence (3) is true, then sentences (1), (2), (6), and (7) are false. Sentence (4) comports with Hinduism's pessimism about life on earth, but not with its pantheism. Sentence (5) accords with the ineffability of pantheism but (5) fails to make all the affirmations of Hinduism.

4. If sentence (4) is true, then sentence (1) is true in that there is no God. However, Buddhism affirms the existence of a sacred realm free of God (Nirvana) that Nietzsche denied. Sentences (2), (3), (6), and (7) are false.

5. If sentence (5) is true, then sentence (5) is true, but we cannot even discern what (5) means, as I argued. If so, we cannot reasonably say it is true. However, the ineffability idea of (5) chimes in with some themes of Hinduism (3).

6. If sentence (6) is true, then sentence (2) is true and half of sentence (7) is true, *There is one God*. The second half, *and Muhammad is his prophet*, is false since Muhammad would have to be a false prophet.

7. If sentence (7) is true, then sentence (2) is true (although Islam rejects Judaism as the final religion) and (1) and (3)-(6) are false.

Of course, there are other religions and worldviews that I have not addressed, and our sentences have only given us a window into the worldview from which they were drawn. Nevertheless, I hope that this short book may have cleared away some conceptual debris and clarified some significant issues related to religion, truth, and logic. If so, I am grateful, and I hope it will assist the reader in the discovery and defense of the truth.

SCRIPTURE INDEX

INTRODUCTIONS IN SEVEN SENTENCES

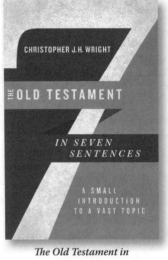

The Old Testament in
Seven Sentences
978-0-8308-5225-3

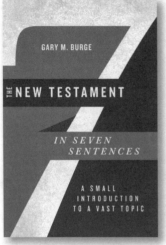

The New Testament in
Seven Sentences
978-0-8308-5476-9

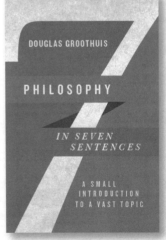

Philosophy in Seven Sentences
978-0-8308-4093-9

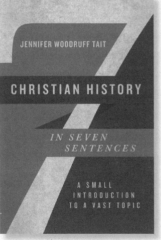

Christian History
in Seven Sentences
978-0-8308-5477-6

ALSO BY DOUGLAS GROOTHUIS

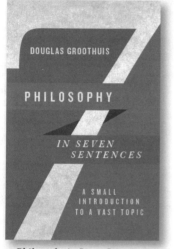

Philosophy in Seven Sentences
978-0-8308-4093-9

Christian Apologetics
978-1-5140-0275-9

Walking Through Twilight
978-0-8308-4518-7